Adult & Continuing Professional Education Practices

Adult & Continuing Professional Education Practices
CPE among Professional Providers

Balan Dass, Ph.D

PARTRIDGE

A Penguin Random House Company

To order additional copies of this book, contact
Toll Free 800 101 2657 (Singapore)
Toll Free 1 800 81 7340 (Malaysia)
orders.singapore@partridgepublishing.com

www.partridgepublishing.com/singapore

DEDICATION

To my parents; Dass @ Manokaran, Thulasi Sinnappan

Brothers', teachers', and friends':

Who taught me lessons in life, as an

Adult and Continuing educate

FOREWORD

The leaders of professions and the public have always assumed that professionals would maintain their competence by continuing to learn throughout their careers. Since the 1960s formal continuing education programs as an approach to learning have increased dramatically so there are now multiple providers. The major types of providers are workplaces, professional associations, higher education, and for-profit agencies. These four organizational contexts shape the type and quality of continuing education offered and it is essential to develop a research base that explains this relationship. Dr. Balan Dass has conducted a research study that offers fresh insights into the contextual factors associated with continuing professional education (CPE) practices at nine institutions in Malaysia. His in-depth study found that four factors influence the type of quality of continuing education offered: the importance of CPE, the ownership of CPE, the planning process, and the collaborative relationships used to develop programs. Given that the development of CPE in Malaysia is in a relatively early stage, it is not surprising that he found the most providers do not have policies and practices that are well-formed for CPE programs. This research is important not only to scholars and leaders in Malaysia, but also because it contributes to the knowledge base for understanding the global context for CPE. Although the growth of CPE is a global phenomenon, the most articulated systems and the research base have been developed in the Global North, such as Canada, Europe, Australia, and the United States. Thus, studies such as this help us understand the similarities and difference among providers in well-established CPE systems and those that are in the early stages of development.

Ronald M. Cervero, PhD
Associate Vice President for Instruction and Professor
University of Georgia
Athens, GA
USA

CONTENTS

Dedication v
Foreword..vii

Chapter 1: Introduction 1

Chapter 2: Understanding Continuing Professional Education (CPE)...... 7
    2.1. What is Continuing Professional Education (CPE) 7
    2.2. CPE and Professional Practice.................................... 9
    2.3. Purpose of CPE.. 9
    2.4. CPE and The Professional 12
    2.5. Providers of CPE...13
    2.6. CPE Educators... 20
    2.7. CPE in Malaysia 21

Chapter 3: CPE: A Literature Review 24
    3.1. The Development of CPE.......................................24
    3.2. Workplace Provision 25
    3.3. Distance Education..25
    3.4. Collaboration Between Providers 26
    3.5. Corporatization...27
    3.6. Regulating Professional Practice.............................27
    3.7. Adult and Continuing Education............................27
    3.8. What is Continuing Education 30
    3.9. CPE Concept...32
    3.10. The Need for CPE.. 34
    3.11. Disadvantages to Mandatory Continuing Education............37
    3.12. Advantages to Mandatory Continuing Education 38
    3.13. Continuing Professional Education Unit (CPEU).................41

Chapter 4: CPE and Program Development 42
    4.1. Program Development Framework......................... 42
    4.2. Program Development 44
    4.3. Purpose of Planning... 46
    4.4. Expectations of a Program 47
    4.5. How Are Educational Programs Planned 47
    4.6. Participatory Approaches in Programming............50
    4.7. Planning Models...52
    4.8. The Interactive Model 53
    4.9. CPE Models...55
    4.10. The Update Model 55
    4.11. The Competence Model 57
    4.12. The Performance Model...................................59
    4.13. CPE Practices of Professional Providers.............62
    4.14. CPE and Collaboration...................................67
    4.15. Features of Positive Collaboration 67
    4.16. Personal Factors 68
    4.17. Collaborative Strategies..................................69
    4.18. Contextual Factors Associated with CPE Practice 69
    4.19. CPE Practice..71

Chapter 5: CPE and Planned Change 76
    5.1. Change and CPE 76
    5.2. Intentional Change and Learning 79
    5.3. Studies of Change and Learning 80
    5.4. CPE and the Change Agent 81
    5.5. CPE and Promoting Change............................82
    5.6. Development of a Need for Change 82
    5.7. Zeroing in on the Problem 82
    5.8. Establishing Goals and Intention of Action............83
    5.9. Committing To Action 83
    5.10. Stabilization of Change..................................83
    5.11. CPE and Training..84
    5.12. CPE and Innovation 85

Chapter 6:   CPE, Professionals and Profession..87

    6.1.   The Professionals..87

    6.2.   The Profession..89

Chapter 7:   CPE in Malaysia 91

    7.1.   Profile and CPE Practices of Providers 92

    7.2.   Provider A - Profile..93

    7.3.   Provider A - CPE Practices... 94

    7.4.   Provider B - Profile.. 96

    7.5.   Provider B - CPE Practices... 97

    7.6.   Provider C - Profile 100

    7.7.   Provider C - CPE Practices 101

    7.8.   Provider D - Profile 104

    7.9.   Provider D - CPE Practices 104

    7.10. Provider E - Profile...107

    7.11. Provider E - CPE Practices 108

    7.12. Provider F - Profile... 110

    7.13. Provider F - CPE Practices 111

    7.14. Provider G - Profile 114

    7.15. Provider G - CPE Practices 116

    7.16. Provider H - Profile 118

    7.17. Provider H - CPE Practices 119

    7.18. Provider I - Profile...125

    7.19. Provider I - CPE Practices 126

Chapter 8:   Contextual Factors Associated with CPE Practices..............130

    8.1.   Importance of CPE..132

    8.2.   Ownership of CPE...138

    8.3.   Planning CPE Programs and Updates..................................144

    8.4.   Collaborative Relationship 151

    8.5.   How The Practices Influence the
         Development of CPE in Malaysia.. 156

Chapter 9:   Philosophy of CPE... 157

    9.1.   Professional Function 159

    9.2.   Program Planning and Development 161

    9.3.   Program Administration and Evaluation.............................163

Chapter 10: Conclusions and Implications 166

    10.1. Philosophy of CPE - Importance of CPE 166

    10.2. Professional Functions - Ownership of CPE........................167

    10.3. Program Planning and Development -
           Planning CPE Updates 169

    10.4. Program Administration and Evaluation -
           Collaborative Relationship 170

    10.5. Personal Factors 171

    10.6. Importance of CPE...172

    10.7. Ownership of CPE..173

    10.8. Planning CPE Programs and Updates................................174

    10.9. CPE and Collaborative Relationship 176

References 177

Table 1: Profile of Providers & Source of Document 92
Table 2: Contextual Factors Associated With CPE Practices 131

CHAPTER 1

INTRODUCTION

The 21ˢᵗ century dawns with the prospect of *wawasan* 2020 (vision 2020) for Malaysians, whereby the country would become a developed nation by the year 2020. Inscribed in the mission statement of *wawasan* 2020, the then prime minister of Malaysia, Tun (Dr) Mahathir Mohamad emphasized that without a doubt, people are our ultimate resource. From the 1990's and beyond, Malaysia must give the fullest emphasis possible to the development of their ultimate human resource, and as such human resource programs support the achievement of vision 2020, especially in the following core areas: professionals, sub-professionals, craftsman and artisans, education, training and managerial skills. In this context, change appears to be the one reliable factor that is constant in life. Nowhere does this seem more blatantly evident than within the workplace.

Employees and their organizations face ever increasing rates of change in products and services, the knowledge and expertise required to deliver these products and services, structures, procedures, processes of work, and policies and regulations intended to ensure public safety and confidence. A brochure from the Malaysian Institute of Accountants recently arrived in the mail, announcing in its cover page, "Stay on track with the latest course from MIA." Targeting accounting professionals through their programs of self-study on current trends and issues, this publication implicitly reflects many of the assumptions about lifelong learning that are often fueled by the requirements of regulatory agencies and professions that aim to tie continuing education to licensure, certification, or practice (Stern and Queeney, 1992). They focus on particular technical and professional skills and emphasize the importance of being updated with changes in one's profession (Queeney, 2000). Continuing professional education (CPE) are fields of practice charged with fostering the necessary change to address these ongoing needs.

On the same note, Nowlen (1988, p.23), describes an informational 'update' as a

> "... typically intensive two or three days short course, a single instructor lecturer and lectures to a fairly large groups of business and professional people who sit for long hours in an audiovisual twilight, making never-to-be read notes at rows of narrow tables covered with green baize and appointed with fat binders and sweating pictures of ice waters..."

This picture is universally recognizable to people in any profession as it is criticized for being largely ineffective in improving the performance of the same professionals. Rapid social changes, explosion of research-based knowledge and the technological innovations of today's world, leaders are now seeing the need to continually prepare people for their future years of professional practice through continuing education. Houle (1980) suggested that some notion of continuing learning has been with us since at least the Middle Ages. Although its aim, form and structure have changed over the years, the persistence of the idea itself speaks to the power of lifelong learning in our lives. Nowhere is this more evident than in work related learning and professional practices. Associated at first with education in the professions, there are now few occupations where continuing learning is not recognized as a critical aspect of employment, a trend accelerated by the so called knowledge explosion and the technological revolution that governs us today. (Queeney, 2000).

The very idea of CPE connotes evolving expertise in a world in which practitioner knowledge is quickly rendered out of date by the fast pace of research and scholarship. From this perspective, practitioners need to continually update the toolbox of skills by acquiring new knowledge from experts specializing in various areas. This knowledge is defined within the narrow realm of information, skills, techniques, and strategies that one might consider for use in his or her practice setting. Guided by a kind of functionalist rationality, continuing education becomes a technical process and the continuing educator's role is replete with technological responsibility (Cervero, 1988). In this view of professional development, knowledge is objective, distinct from the practitioners who act on it, and not related to the particular sociocultural contexts in which they work. It is acquired and presumably internalized by the individuals through the programs aimed at transmitting specific knowledge and skills related to the performance of particular work related tasks.

Accordingly, Cervero (2001) in the 1970s began to see embryonic evidence for systems of continuing education in the United States of America. For example:

1. Several professions proposed plans for systems of lifelong professional education.
2. All professions have a system of accreditation for continuing education providers.
3. Billions of dollars are spent on providing and attending continuing education programs.

Given Cervero's (2000) assertion that a major trend in the field of CPE is the amount of CPE offered at the workplace dwarfs that which is offered by any other type of provider, and surpasses that of all other providers combined, coupled with the evidence presented in this book, there can be little doubt that the real world contexts for CPE are drawing closer together. Having said this, according to Cervero (1998), we have yet to implement a practice that recognizes continuing education as an effective tool in today's complex world. The major reason for this lacking of effective continuing education is not for want: the professions are in transitional stages of their socio-economical lives, always experimenting with many different purposes, forms and institutional location for the delivery of continuing education.

These practices, according to Cervero (2001), are as follows:

1. Devoted mainly to updating practitioners about the newest developments.
2. Transmitted in a didactic fashion.
3. Delivered through a pluralistic group of providers, professional associations, non-governmental organizations, professional providers, universities, and
4. They do not work together in any coordinated fashion.

In major professions, such as medicine (Meyer, 1975) and law (Vernon, 1983) and in some minor professions such as librarianship (Stone, 1986), professionals have acknowledged their commitment to CPE. The term 'continuing' assumes that there is some further development of initial training, a smooth transition within and subsequent career progress. However, even a cursory glance at the practices of CPE suggests profound discontinuity of emphasis and tradition, separate personnel, and different structures and modes of organization that spreads far from its original intent.

The greatest influences on CPE are the histories and current trajectories of the professions. These indicate that the distinctive features claimed for professional workers include:

1. A body of formal knowledge acquired through professional education required for membership and sustained by CPE. However, such knowledge is now recognized as being mostly necessary but far from sufficient, hence the recent emphasis on competencies that are learned on the job for professionals as well as other workers, and the continuing debate about the nature of the relationship between theory and practice.

2. Authority based on specialist knowledge and expertise. When professions are very powerful, like law and medicine, their authority is very strong within their own domains. However, weak professions can only assert collective negative power on a few contentious issues.

3. Accountability to their clients through adherence to a professional code of conduct, which normally covers both ethical principles and obligations to maintain competence through ongoing learning. On the positive side, the professions additional learning programs, networks, and resources are governed to those provided by the employers. Employers often see the more powerful professions as a rival source of power and authority, which might divert professional learning efforts away from their own priorities.

Among the reasons, much more is involved than just updating a body of knowledge. The development of personal competency is of equal importance. We all learn by doing, by our success and mistakes. We establish one's mastery of the new conceptions of one's own profession, to grow as a person as well as a professional. Houle (1980) suggested that professional competency could be developed and improved by the process of continuing professional education. Through this process, the professional such as management, human resource and training is able to continue to refine the standards that characterize its work.

Professionals have long recognized that traditional professional training cannot fully meet the needs of the individuals or the needs of the organizations in a rapidly changing world. Studying for the award of a professional qualification at the beginning of a career provides a valuable base for the individual.

It cannot, however, do more than ensure the acquisition of knowledge and expertise, which is relevant at the time the qualification is obtained. Qualification studies of this kind still have an important role to play but as part of a wider learning and development process. This process needs to be 'owned' by the individual and utilizes a much wider range of learning opportunities than formal, off the job training.

The question of how does knowledge become meaningful in professional practice comes to the mind of the professional more often than not. We do know that over the course of their lives, professionals develop an integrated, holistic knowledge framework that is used in the context of the service they provide to clients. We have also established that this knowledge and practice is often developed from CPE programs, from conversations, discussions with colleagues and from experience in professional practices (Cervero 1988). The issue of professional practice within the field of adult education is crucial to the various stakeholders. Employers and professionals spend billions of dollars annually on CPE programs. In the United States of America, a further USD180billion per year is spent on informal, on-the-job training (Rowden,1996). Despite this huge investment in CPE programs, the field of adult education can offer few assurances that the knowledge and skill learned within these programs are linked to the context of professional practice.

Professionals develop and change their practice with the intent of continually meeting clients' needs and expectations. However, most professionals go through this process of professional development without a clear understanding of how knowledge learned in CPE becomes meaningful in practice. Although the stages of professional development have been described (Benner, 1984;

Dreyfus & Dreyfus, 1986), the learning process underlying professional development and the connection to the context of practice has not been articulated. For professionals to continue meeting the needs of their clients, a greater understanding of the connections between the context of practice and professional learning is needed.

CHAPTER 2

UNDERSTANDING CONTINUING PROFESSIONAL EDUCATION (CPE)

What is Continuing Professional Education (CPE)

Concept of continuing professional education (CPE) has evolved over the years. Queeny, (2000) described that during the middle ages, CPE has been known as staff development, management, or professional development. At that time of industrialization, chambers of commerce would have labeled 9CPE) as a sought of apprenticeship or guild system, whereby, candidates go through a guided (CPE) system, before the candidates are certified to undertake a profession or semi-profession. The process of continuing professional education only took shape in the late 1960s', whereby a systematic form of lifelong education was found evident with the physician's profession.

According to Cervero; (2000) & Dryer;(1962), from these conceptualization process therein to support the physicians, quickly emerged the process of re-licensure and re-certification during the seventies. Cervero & Azzaretto (1990) propounded that over the next two decades numerous professions would have adopted the philosophy of continuing professional education for their employees. Cervero (1988), Jarvis (1995), also described (CPE) as a popular process to update adults in their particular profession, and these can be labeled as education permanente, lifelong learning, or re-current education.

Experts in adult learning have further defined continuing professional education (CPE) as they have perceived it. Houle (1980), refers to CPE as continuing learning while Cervero (1988), sees CPE as a significant area of educational activity. Apps (1979), defines CPE as further enhancing the development of human abilities after entrance into employment It includes in service, upgrading and updating education. Knox, (1989) propounded that CPE is seen as a systematic process of learning and preparing the candidate for the field of practice, which includes maintaining proficiency of knowledge and skill as practiced by the candidate. This is a step for practitioners to evolve professionally and progress from being a novice to being an expert

CPE is continuing because learning never ceases, regardless of age or seniority. It is professional because it is focused on personal competence in a professional role; and it is concerned with education because its goal is to improve personal performance and enhance career progression. Many aspects of CPE are not new - most professionals have always recognized the need for professional updating; but CPE's emphasis on systematic development and the comprehensive identification of learning opportunities now provides a framework within which formal and informal learning activities can be set. Learning and development becomes planned, rather than accidental. CPE is a field of practice and study that is directed towards the ongoing needs of professionals as subscribed by Cervero, (2001). Hence, the purpose of CPE is to certify and improve professional knowledge and practice. Much of the foundational thinking for CPE was first introduced during the 1980's. For example, Houle (1980) initially described professionals as:

> "Men and women... deeply versed in advanced and subtle bodies of knowledge, which they apply with dedication in solving complex practical problems. They learn to study, apprenticeship, and experience, both by expanding their comprehension of formal disciplines and by finding new ways to use them to achieve specific ends, constantly moving forward and backward from theory and practice so that each enriches the other. Such people protect one another and are sometimes extended special protection by society far beyond that granted to other citizens. The price of protection is vigilance against poor performance and unethical behavior, and that vigilance is exercised by the privileged person, by others of similar specialization, and by society..."

CPE and Professional Practice

Cervero (1988), characterized professionals as business, service or community oriented leaders that apply a systematic body of knowledge to problems that are highly relevant to the central values of society, and Schon (1983) stated that professional activity consists of instrumental problem solving made rigorous by the application of scientific theory and technique. Professionals define the social problems with which they deal and, by extension, actually define societal needs. For example, teachers decide the curriculum and physicians decide both the diagnosis and the cure (Cervero, 1988). Although there is no consensus on the criteria that define a professional, a popular approach among adult educators is to consider all occupations existing on a continuum of professionalization (Cervero, 1988; Houle, 1980).

Purpose of CPE

Various views on the purpose of CPE exist, but the functionalist view has the deepest roots and the strongest following in America. According to this view, the purpose of CPE, is to help professionals provide higher quality service to clients by improving their knowledge, competence, or performance (Cervero, 1988). In addition to helping professionals, CPE also plays the important role of certifying professional knowledge. Queeney (2000) identified three components of a competent professional practice:

(a) Knowledge of a body of information,
(b) The use of that knowledge in a skill, and
(c) Performance that applies the knowledge and skill within the context of practice.

So, individuals engage in CPE to learn the changing knowledge in their ever-changing professions, and certification publicly acknowledges this learning (Knox, 1989). Individuals than create new knowledge by applying their learning and by constructing meaning through reflection about the lived experience of their practice (Daley, 2001).

When professionals practice with a view to progressively build on existing knowledge and not merely find solutions, they inadvertently subscribe to the personal mastery model (Senge 1990; Fritz 1991) and professional artistry (Schon, 1987). The fundamental approach to helping professionals to think beyond the predictable outcome is a compelling vision that requires deep thinking, as well as the benefit of unplanned learning opportunities available to professionals (Schon, 1987). For effective practice Schon's (1987) professional artistry is in the application of knowledge, that knowing is in the action of professionals not arising from a planned course of action nor can they state a rule or reason for their judgments. Often, practitioners do not overcome situations merely by knowing-in-action; they reconstruct the situation or problem to make it solvable from their repertoire of experiences. Effective practice in continuing professional education does not exist in isolation from the real world of practice. Practitioners cannot merely afford to apply standardized solutions but must be able to apply them through a quarum of situations.

This critical viewpoint rejects rigid prescriptions for the exemplary practice of a professional (Cervero, 1988). A contextual understanding of the situations is urged. The critical viewpoint emphasizes the need to continually construct new choices that make professional practice effective. Ideal practices, which produce specific results, are realities for controlled situations. But professional practice is known to be conducted in a context composed of varying personalities, planning expectations, conflicting goals and limited resources. Good professional practice is not judged by prescribed knowledge or discrete guidelines but by an understanding of why professionals do what they do and when they do it. But in Schon's (1987) contention, it is inadequate that practitioners merely posses declarative knowledge. Professionals need to excel in their field as experts The appropriate knowledge needed for effective practitioners is to know how to connect continuous learning, plans, techniques, ideas and knowledge to make judgment in the uncertain and often changing contexts of practice or indeterminate areas of higher level learning.

Daley, (2001) describes this as linking knowledge to practice. Higher-level learning comes about only through dilemmas that an individual is confronted with where a progressively intolerable conflict of central elements in business theory is in use (Schon, 1975, p. 8). Learning is generated when the individual reflects upon his assumptions, actions and distinguishes them from his intended or espoused actions. The emerging mismatch is a disparity or the gap. The ability to recognize and correct this disparity helps professionals to become more explicit that then set them on a learning trail.

Professionals who are unaware of their own shortcomings often fail to excel. They are unable to create a process of dialogue or art of inquiring with themselves. They try to understand why they are predisposed to learning in a particular way, their personal cognitive style. Argyris and Schon's (1996) process of knowing in Model II provides a realistic abstraction of the actual experiences of professionals in the following steps:

1) They gather valid information from practice;
2) They exercise free and informed choices on practices;
3) They exhibit an internal commitment to their chosen course of action;
4) While constantly monitoring its implementation. Which means individuals must reflect critically upon their practice;
5) They make preferred choices and commit to act upon them; and
6) They evaluate their decisions. That is, deliberate action must follow for without action there is no learning (Pedler, 1997).

Action learning (Revans, 1982; Pedler, 1997; Mumford, 1997) is a development approach that treats the task itself as learning, as an opportunity for individuals to reflect and make progress on their problems while working at their tasks. Literature reviewed (O'Neil, 1999)proposes that action learning fall under four broad schools of thought: scientific, critical reflection, experiential and tacit.

In the tacit (Polanyi, 1967) school, individuals are expected to learn incidentally - learning is not structured. Learning opportunities present themselves when they work on real problems. Learning from experience may not also be intentionally designed into learning programs. But scientific and critical reflection advocates the use of learning coaches and mentors.

To achieve excellence, greater capacity to learn from experience, higher-level performance, a sustained reflection in action through the various levels of learning is needed. Individuals who become aware of their own inability to perform up to expectation or realize their disparity between their intended action and actual behavior would challenge the status quo. They would modify their governing values that relate to realizing transformational needs. Individuals' approach to learning would then be more systematic. Professional education, be it for the betterment of practice or higher levels of development, suffers from being too theoretical (Lester, 1995), while the schools of practical knowledge confine their curriculum to solving theunpredictable argument that is not in the equilibrium of theory and practice, but to adequately prepare professionals to solve real life problems. The movement is in the change from the post industrial to the present information base (Schon, 1971; Ackoff, 1974) that professionals and practitioners develop. It is the uncertain and indeterminate areas that pose the greatest challenge to professionals. Hence it is said that when professionals make sense of a situation, they reconcile, integrate, or choose among conflicting appreciations of a situation so as to construct a coherent problem worth solving (Schon, 1987).

Schon's (1987) reflective practices send a powerful message that professionals need to move beyond any rational model to one that builds a relationship between the epistemology of "how do we know" and reflective practices. While, the flexible preposition to a new epistemology of learning is 'reflecting in action' (Schon, 1987) varying forms of Schon's reflective practice has complimented the field of professional practice. In Lester's (1995) model of "Reflecting, Inquiring, Creating", she suggests how professionals should excel beyond mere acquisition of knowledge and competence as in Model A, to transforming practices to a higher level of performance as that in Model B. The Model of Reflecting, Inquiring and Creating involves critical thinking in a new personal theory and changes to one's own practice. The model operates at a deep thinking level akin to "double-loop" learning (Argyris) in which practitioners assumptions and theory in use are assessed in change.

CPE and The Professional

Society's principal business is conducted through professionals' specially trained to carry out that business, be it waging a war and defending the country, educating the children, diagnosing and curing diseases, judging and punishing those who violate the law, managing industries and businesses, and designing and constructing buildings. Formal institutions like schools, hospitals, courts of law, and many others are areas for the exercise of professional activity.

Professionals are called upon to define and solve problems, and it is through them that we strive for social progress.

Therefore a professional can be defined as an individual who is engaged in a professional activity or vocation as a remunerated occupation, and needs to attend CPE programs to renew their certificate to practice and also to meet the minimum standard requirement of the organization which they hold the professional membership. As such, professionals involve the application of general principles to specific problems, and it is a feature of modern societies that such general principles are abundant and growing. A professional's profession is a highly specialized occupation that involves practicing the substantive field of knowledge that the specialist professes to command and the technique of production or application of knowledge over which the specialist claims mastery (Schon, 1996).

Providers of CPE

By the end of the 1980's according to Cervero (1988), professional providers have also seen widespread talk of a 'new paradigm' for industrial and commercial enterprises. At the core are notions of employee involvement, commitment and flexibility in roles and organization structure giving meaningful and responsible task, utilizing CPE and the profession.

A clear definition of professions is elusive. Becker (1962) examined the efforts of social scientists since 1900 to define the term "professional" and concluded that no one definition or set of occupations can be acceptable to all. A list of characteristics developed by (Flexner, 1915), who believed that there are certain objective standards that can be formulated which aid in distinguishing one profession from the other occupation. He identified the following six characteristics as essential for occupations to claim professional status. Professions must:

    (1) Involve intellectual operations,

    (2) Derive their material from science,

    (3) Involve definite and practical ends,

    (4) Possess an educationally communicable technique,

    (5) Tends towards self organization, and

(6) Be altruistic.

Today many occupations are applying these generic criteria to decide whether their occupation is a profession. This process is called the static approach because objective criterion firmly discriminates between those occupations that are inherently a profession and those that are not. On the other hand, the process approach came to full being when (Vollmer and Mills, 1966) used it as organized principle for their book on professionalization.

This approach viewed all occupations as existing on a continuum of professionalization. Another possibility raised by the process approach is that occupations can deprofessionalise, suggesting that the continuum is not a one-way street. An assumption of the process approach is that there is no clear-cut boundary separating professions from occupations. Vollmer and Mills (1966) stated that professionalization is a process that may affect any occupation to a greater or lesser degree. Cervero (1988) argues that occupations in England and United States have sought to be classified as professions since the late nineteenth century. He further notes that the newer occupations:

> "...did not seek classification as professions to gain status and justify a market shelter; such an umbrella title imputing special institutional characteristics to them was not employed to distinguish them, rather, the status and security of these occupations were gained by other means, such as protections provided by their governments..."

This approach contrasts dramatically with both static and process approaches in that it assumes there is no such thing as an ideal profession and that no set of criteria is necessarily associated with it. Cervero (1988) argues that such a definition takes as central the fact that 'profession' is an honorific title...a collective symbol and one that is highly valued. Cervero (1988) proposes that for an occupation to be classified as a profession, some amount of higher education must be a prerequisite to employment. The rationale is that formal knowledge creates qualification for particular jobs, from which others who lack qualification are routinely excluded. Such a circumstance is likely to mean that those occupations have developed a coherent organization that succeeds in carving out a labor – market shelter.

During the 1930s when Flexner offered these criteria, distinctions between professions and vocations were no doubt easier to recognize. Only a few vocations, such as medicine, law, clergy, teaching, and, to some extent, architecture and engineering, were commonly thought of as professions. Today many vocations can claim they are professions within Flexner's definition. This is a result of the *zeitgeist* for professionalization during the late nineteenth and early twentieth century that encouraged all occupations to become professions (Apps, 1985). Houle offered an approach to categorizing professions involving thirteen dynamic processes rather than static characteristics. His scheme recognized that professions, even the established ones, are always in a state of professionalizing (Houle, 1980). Houle's method was not meant to draw a clear line between professions and non-professions but did provide an index as to the degree of professionalization.

Despite the difficulty in defining the professions, there is no lack of critics who have suggestions for their improvement. Professions and aspiring professions have drawn critical review because of their special contract with society. They pledge to provide needed services in a responsible manner in return for control over their areas of expertise. Concern over the special status and privileges given to professionals have long existed, but in recent years this arrangement has been questioned. Illich (1979) retorted that as a form of public entertainment, pestering professionals is hardly new. What is new about this current phase is its less genial mood, and its more jugular objective.

The attack on the professions peaked in the 1970s when books such as Illich's, " The Disabling Professions", and "Lieberman's Tyranny of the Expert", were widely read. These writers and their cohorts described the professions as morally corrupt institutions, which were beyond redemption. Schon (1996) countered this claim by pointing out that much of the movement for reform and moral revitalization during this period came from within the professions. He further suggested that professionals generally reflect prevailing values more than they battle to overcome them, and added that they may accelerate cultural trends in progress, but when they do, they are likely to use institutional channels that follow the lay of the land .

Other less critical concerns for the professions have also emerged during the last two decades. As early as 1980, Houle recognized that modern professional practice was changing from one-on-one with clients to a more collective work environment which would require greater skill in team work and project management (Houle, 1980). Current trends in managed health care attest to this shift in professional culture among physicians.

While this may be a new phenomenon to some professions, it has been a common characteristic of architectural practice for over a century. Architects typically work in teams or direct teams that comprised of a variety of consultants and other architects. This is an area in which the study of architectural practice may contribute to other professions. Another expressed concern for the professions is their apparent lack of interdisciplinary efforts and leadership directed toward solving societal problems (Nasseh, 1999). Cervero (1988) too, charged that professions could better serve society by engaging in a constant critical review of their practices.

The call for professions to take on more leadership and to be more reflective is indicative of an important characteristic of professions that is missing from Flexner's definition. According to Nasseh (1999), true professions have a covenant with society in which they accept responsibility to serve the best interests of society in return for special privileges and status.

Nasseh (1999) traced the origin of this covenant to the first true profession in America - the ministry. The word profession as we now use it evolved from the action of ministers *professing* their commitment to selfless service to the church. They argued that the professions of law, the professorate, and medicine acquired some of the attributes and status of the ministry as they emerged in the later half of the 19th century. It is this calling to selfless service that separates professions from vocations.

Finally, true professions are self-referenced sub cultures. Members of each profession hold a unique set of common values and speak a special language not easily understood by outsiders (Cervero, 1988). As defined by Nowlen (1988), professional culture is the context within which individual meaning - making and personal growth take place. Nowlen described the factors affecting professional performance as a double helix of a professional's personal history intertwined with the professional culture.

This concept is supported by emerging theories of organizational learning that suggest that members of an organization and the organization itself can learn and that this learning is affected by organizational structure and climate (Senge, 1990). Nowlen's concept has special significance for continuing professional education and this book. It suggested that understanding change and learning in the professions must include the perspective of individual professionals; and, the study of continuing professional education must recognize the unique cultural influences of each profession.

Cervero (1988) characterized professions as service or community oriented occupations that apply a systematic body of knowledge to problems that are highly relevant to the central values of society, and Schon (1983) stated that professional activity consists of instrumental problem solving made rigorous by the application of scientific theory and technique. As these descriptions highlight, professions define the social problems with which they deal and by extension, actually define societal needs. For example, teachers decide the curriculum, and the physicians decide both the diagnosis and the cure (Cervero, 1989). Although there is no consensus on the criteria that define a profession, a popular approach among adult educators is to consider all occupations existing on a continuum of professionalization (Cervero, 1988; Houle, 1980) while developing their skills, often in the context of product and focused teamwork. As the trend moves into the 1990's, we find that research in the field of work organization demand developments in theory and practice. Professional providers have changed from their historic origin. They are 'updating' their members on the awareness and happenings around them. For professional members, they find that the updating process is like an 'awareness' of current knowledge, rediscovery and reexamining change. According to the literature search, some of the major providers of CPE are extension schools in the universities, professional associations, non – profit organizations, employing agencies and independent providers. Cervero (1988, p.77) offered the following description of CPE providers,

> "…at a minimum continuing professional education appears
> to be a complex of instructional systems, many of them heavily

didactic, in which people who know something teach it those
who do not know it. The central aim of such teaching, which
is offered by many providers, is to keep professionals up to date
in their practice..."

CPE programs can be sponsored by professional schools or by university wide
CPE units. Houle (1980) describes the various ways in which professional
schools and universities relate: there are many kinds and levels of such schools,
some are free standing and others are parts of larger entities, often universities.
A major reason that professional schools sponsors CPE programs is because it
often generates a revenue surplus, which can be used to fund other university
projects. The programming function can be performed only by individuals who
are trained in the specific profession. As such, continuing educators - rather
than faculty heads or clients - tend to be the central figures in the planning
process (Cervero, 1988). These continuing educators, because they understand
their profession, academically and from practice tend not to rely on others for
programming ideas.

Universities are considered as a good CPE provider because their research
strength are a source of knowledge for most professions. It is only appropriate
that faculty members who originally develop and present this information
should teach it to practitioners through CPE programs (Smutz, Crowe, and
Lindsay, 1986). Universities too, are experienced with lengthy and complex
forms on instruction which lead to certification of CPE units upon successful
completion of such programs (Cruse, 1983; Houle 1980). At the same time
it must be acknowledged that universities have many physical facilities as
compared to other providers, such as housing, libraries, meeting rooms,
computer rooms and food service (Bloom, 1983; Houle, 1980).

Professional associations are also providers of CPE programs. Most of the
professions are represented by their respective associations. Professional
associations deliver CPE programs in different ways, depending on the number
of members, the scope of purpose, and the size and structure of the staff. The
educational programs sponsored by the professional association that are defined
as instruction are conferences, convention training programs, publications and
training workshops (Houle, 1980).

Cervero (1988) emphasizes that a study showed that all associations provided some form of CPE programs for their members, and one-third sponsored certificate, licensure, or degree programs. Professional associations too have the ability to secure a wide array of talent from their membership and therefore bring about a variety of points of view to the educational programming (Cevero, 1988 Houle, 1980: Puetz, 1985; Suleiman, 1983).

Additionally, associations are best at sponsoring conferences, and have direct access to professionals who are seeking CPE and are familiar with their learning needs (Cruse, 1983; Suleiman, 1983). Lastly, associations are able to engage in cost-effective strategies for delivering educational programs. Professional associations have their weakness too. Some being that the organization may lack physical facilities, libraries, food service, staff and marketing expertise. Moreover some of the programs run may not be the latest and could well be considered by members as out dated. Furthermore staff members cannot take the leadership role as they are considered to be of assistance to the professional committee members. Staff are often viewed as simply 'seminar schedulers' (Hohmann, 1980). Directors of education who have many fold responsibilities have limitation to their leadership role in the program development process. As such when the board changes from year to year, long term planning or future oriented programming suffers (Hohmann, 1980).

Another provider of CPE programs is employers. Employers such as hospitals, social agencies, business firms and government bodies offer tremendous amount of CPE to their employees. It is estimated that the CPE programs sponsored by the employers surpasses sixty billion annually (Cevero, 1988; Eurich, 1985). The important task of educators in the employments setting is to improve participants' performance with respect to the need of the agency, which eventually could be remedied (Houleand Craig, 1980). In the employers setting, the needs of the agency could be identified directly and program planning can be done according to the need analyzed, and can be conducted in the work setting as applied training in the workplace. On the same note, programs are planned and scheduled with minimum time lost, thus pleasing the employers. On the other hand it must be noted that during difficult times, employers slash their training budget. Nowlen in Cervero (1988) also states that employers seldom have professionals in charge of education, thus the educational planning is far less proficient against their organizational goals.

Independent providers represent a wide range of agencies or institutions and constitute a growing segment of the field (Suleiman, 1980). These providers operate on a profit basis, others on a non-profit. Cooperatives, self-help ventures and philanthropic organizations also fall into this wide category. Suleiman (1980) argues that the greatest advantage that independent providers have is program development. These providers respond to learner's need quickly; with good instruction, free from problems of faculty involvement, committee approvals and other political considerations.

According to Houle (1980), most private providers offer their programs nationally, and thus amortize their development cost. Because of their flexibility, independent providers have pioneered new formats and methods of instruction that have subsequently been adopted by larger and better-established providers of CPE. On the other hand independent providers lack quality and image and this makes them less credible. Houle (1980) notices that, many independent providers have exploited either professionals desire to learn or their need to meet recertification requirements with programs that have promised more than they have delivered.

Independent providers are also extremely sensitive to economic downturn when only few participants attend the programs, thus making a loss. Furthermore, these provider slack the facilities necessary for extensive educational programming, library facilities and conducive training environment to make CPE programs a success.

CPE Educators

CPE programs are conducted by CPE educators, who are independent agents serving their audience in an appropriate way. The organization demands that the CPE educator knows his subject matter so that they can deliver effectively. According to Cervero (1988), CPE educators must be sensitive to how their effort contributes to the organizational goals. CPE educators practice in different agencies and have different educational functions. Some organization use continuing education as a means to improve performance of professionals while others use it as a public relations strategy. For CPE educators to survive and prosper, they must keep in mind the educational goals of the organization and be effective in fulfilling it. Cervero and Simerly(1988) noticed that no matter what type of agency continuing educators working; the leadership challenge is to position CPE activities so that they come to be seen as actively contributing to the institutional goals.

CPE in Malaysia

In order to keep up with change, individuals and organizations must develop new skills and be innovative. Continuing professional education is playing a crucial role in the lives of many professionals as they adapt to rapidly changing work environments. There can be few professionals who have been unaffected by the rapid pace of change which has influenced the professions over the past decade. Professionalism relies increasingly on an ability to respond quickly to changing market conditions, to client requirements and to the influences of the government policies. We are all being encouraged to embrace change and foster innovation. To adapt to these changes, it demands new skills. No longer can keeping "up-to-date" be optional; it is increasingly central to professional and organizational success. The response of many professionals to this challenge has been to embrace the concept of continuing professional education.

Vision 2020, first mooted by Prime Minister YAB Datuk Seri Dr.Mahathir Mohammed in 1990 was initially received with reservation. Since then, Malaysians have now understood the concept our former Prime Minister was advocating and are committed towards helping the nation achieve developed nation status by the year 2020. Human resource development has emerged as the crucial driving force towards realizing the goals of Vision 2020.

We not only need to acquire skills and knowledge but we also need to instill correct work attitudes and ethics. A disciplined and skillful workforce will no doubt lead to increased productivity and ensure that our economic development is both resilient and sustainable in the long term. Several approaches and modules may be adopted to develop our human resource sector.

However several core factors will first have to be addressed to ensure the success of our human resource development program:

1. Education; including technical and vocational, science and technology, computer related and robotics technology
2. Entrepreneurship and entrepreneurial development
3. Appropriate mix between professional, sub-professional, craftsman and artisans
4. Marketing skills
5. Correct work culture, attitude and ethics

Towards this juncture, skills upgrading, capital deepening, technology development and organizational improvements will underpin the transformation of the economy towards productivity driven growth. With a high proportion of the labor force in the young age group, investments in human capital to increase skills and knowledge of workers will enable each unit of labor to deliver more output or higher value-added products. Accelerated skill development programmes under the seventh Malaysia plan will improve the supply of technically proficient manpower and expertise. With a better quality workforce, the learning curve and gestation period associated with the application of more advanced automation systems and the acquisition of new knowledge will be shortened.

During this plan period, the principal thrust of human resource development efforts will be the preparation of a strong human resource base for long-term economic growth and global competition. Given the shift towards a productivity-driven economy, the emphasis will be on increasing the efficiency of labor utilization and greater capital and technology intensity in production. A productivity-driven economy will require higher levels of professional and skilled manpower as well as administrative expertise. In this regard, the upgrading of skills and knowledge of the labor force, promotion of managerial competence and initiative as well as advancement of scientific and technological know-how, will be pursued only through continuing professional education to all concerned.

At the Malaysian Society for Training and Development, Asean Conference and Exhibition (STAR Publication, 1996, p.5) Dato' Paduka Rafidah Aziz, delivering her keynote address emphasized that, "…training of trainers so that those responsible for the nations human resource development are themselves adequately equipped with the latest information, knowledge and expertise to upgrade and enhance the skills and capabilities of the nation's workforce".

On another occasion, during the annual dinner of the Malaysian Institute of Estate Agents (2000), the President urged the members of the institute to update themselves with the latest information on real estate law, taxation, property valuation and foreign investment ruling. This is to enable the agents to provide professional advice to would be buyers or investors.

In 2001, at a council meeting of the Malaysian Institute of Chartered Secretaries, the council president reminded members of the fraternity to update themselves with the latest information of their vocation. The time has come to face the global challenges of Asia Free Trade Zone(AFTA) and World Trade Organisation(WTO). This simply means that members must be familiar with international laws, financial investments laws and other rulings or information much needed by the clients.

With the rapid changes taking place in the world, continuing professional education has a direct relationship in safeguarding the capital resources of the country. Professionals in the various professional bodies, by enhancing themselves with the latest up-dates, provide professional advice on the latest information to make timely decisions by the valued clients who would be investing millions of dollars in this country.

CHAPTER 3

CPE: A LITERATURE REVIEW

In our increasingly complex society, where the boundaries of knowledge are expanding rapidly, there are professions with many professionals within each group. Whilst the expertise that they provide is highly valued, their clients are now more knowledgeable, more discerning and therefore expect much more in terms of service and quality. The dual pressures of increased competition and client's high expectations combined with a whole range of social, political, commercial and technological factors are driving profound changes in the ways that professional work is organized, regulated and rewarded. These changes are forcing professional providers, professional associations and non-government organizations to reassess their roles and structures, their relationship amongst each other, and towards their members and the society at large.

The next decade will see further growth in the number of professionals, as more people gain college degrees and professional level qualifications as well as associate professionals, such as nurses and legal executives, attain full professional status. The rapid growth of the professions, from a small, elite and privileged group in the 60's, to a large diverse occupational group in the millennium, will provide major educational and developmental challenges for professional providers, professional associations, educational establishments and employers to educate her members.

The Development of CPE

Formalized systems for Continuing Professional Education first began to emerge in the 1960s- the first clear signal of the new view was the publication in 1962 of a conceptual scheme for the lifelong education of physicians. It was not until the 1970s that CPE became rigueur, initially as a basis for re-licensure and recertification rather than improvement (Cervero and Azzaretto, 1990). By the 1980s, organized and comprehensive continuing education programs were widespread amongst the longer-established professions like engineering, accounting, law, medicine, pharmacy, veterinary medicine, social work, librarianship, architecture, nursing home administration, nursing management and many more other professions (Cervero, 1988). During that decade, systems of accreditation were developed by many professions (Kenny,1985). The 1990s provided us with a picture of a single instructor lecturing large groups of professionals recognized as continuing education, and to date we do not have a system of CPE that is effective in today's complex world - the reason being that CPE and the professions are in a transitional stage. Testing whether or not this is the case is clearly made difficult by the lack of information on existing CPE and the ephemeral nature of many of the learning systems. Despite this there are five major trends that we can identify which can help point to the future of CPE.

Workplace Provision

The first of these trends is that the amount of CPE offered at the workplace is far larger than that being offered by any other provider, including professional associations. Raw statistics may show the proportion of income spent on education by companies to be very low, often as little as 1%. The true picture of time spent training staff for better practice is much harder to reach, and must be much higher, probably anything up to 10%. In any event, it is likely that company-provided CPE dwarfs all the other provision types put together, and it is also the most rapidly growing technique. In 1992, for instance, the annual increase of training hours provided by firms was the equivalent to the teaching load of some state universities (Cervero, 2000).

Distance Education

While some CPE organizations have long been accustomed to teaching professionals in their home even before rise of the Internet, there can be no doubt that the communications revolution is the principal force behind the recent shift in the nature of CPE. The advent of fairly universal access has increased ease of provision and changed its style almost beyond recognition. At first professional associations and other bodies who did not have the firms' advantage of direct contact with the learners adopted these new techniques. As time passed, this distinction has been eroded by the increasing use of online learning facilities within companies, as exemplified by the creation of corporate universities. The Virtual University provides students with a choice of 1600 courses and 100 complete degree or certificate programs ("California Spins..." 1998). Professional associations are also major providers of continuing education. Education is a major, if not the primary function of associations. In a recent study of 5,500 national associations by the Hudson Institute on behalf of the American Society of Association Executives (Maurer and Sheets, 1998), it was found that 90percent of associations offer continuing education to their members and the public, spending an estimated $8.5 billion to offer courses on technical, scientific and business practices.

Collaboration Between Providers

At the same time as CPE had been rapidly developing, policy movements have put universities under pressure to better aid their local economies. It is only natural therefore that many universities should enter into CPE provisions in collaboration with the other bodies. In fact, these associations have now become the norm – about 90% of education offered by US employers are developed in collaboration rather than in-house. The corresponding figure for professional associations (again, the United States) is appropriately smaller (around 50%) as these organizations have a tradition of developing their own scheme. Even for-profit training groups have become willing to share their technology infrastructure and marketing skills in exchange for better content from other institutions. Accompanying such collaborations, in the age of globalized markets, are a quantity of international agreements between similar groups in different countries (Cervero, 1988).

Corporatization

CPE has historically often been used as a moneymaking venture: the for-profit training organizations of the modern era are an obvious demonstration of this. Professional associations or universities have traditionally used the revenues generated from CPE to support some of those institutions' other activities. This phenomenon has certainly become more pronounced as time has passed, with many private education providers conglomerating into sizeable firms. In addition, corporate universities (Cervero, 1988) spun off from larger companies are now so developed that they are generating their own revenues for those firms.

Regulating Professional Practice

Since the 1960s, the standards demanded of professional in public life have been steadily increasing. This issue, which is effectively faced by the professional associations alone, provoked the development of accountability mechanisms. A favorite method used to increase accountability is CPE, in systems where professional licenses will not be reissued until certain CPE targets have been met (Collins, 1998). It has been argued that this method only serves as a rubber stamp, and actually does little to increase the competency of its practitioners. Even so, the number of professions using this technique has been rising steadily for many years. The above is the backdrop of the last 20 years of CPE. From the backdrop of firm-dominated schemes, through the rise of distance learning to the increasingly commercial and collaboration provisions of CPE, we can see the patterns that have shaped the state of CPE today.

Adult and Continuing Education

When viewed in a broader context, education includes both youths and adults. If it is agreed that the educational process must continue throughout the life of the individual, then it is impossible to argue that there is an age set aside for education (Lengrand 1975).

Recent trends have indicated that more adults, who have been out of school, are involved in education. This trend is a result of social change, much of it associated with demographic and economic development (Long 1983).

Some of these developments include the changing of age profile, rising educational levels throughout the American society, greater interest in the rights of special population, shifting attitudes towards work, increasing frequency of career and occupational change, occupational adolescence, mandatory continuing education, increasing acceptance of non-traditional approaches to education, and finally changing expectations and the expansion of education (Long 1983).

In discussing adult education, scholars often mention the definition of adulthood, adult and continuing education that involves adults. At first glance, there may be nothing confusing about the notion of adulthood but, when the term has been translated into legislative terms and budgetary provisions made, difficulties are encountered (Boshier1983). Boshier (1983) further noted that in many countries, an adult is a person who has reached an age which may range from 17 to 21 years.

The field of adult education has complication in its understanding. It is known by many other names. Even the term adult education, which once described the field, is being replaced by such terms as continuing education, recurrent education, lifelong education, and human resource development (Stubblefield 1981).

In fact to this list, other terms can be added, such as permanent education, non-traditional education, community education, andragogy, and extension education. It has not won universal acceptance by those with the education of adults (Darkenwald & Merriam 1982).

The most often used synonym is "continuing education" (Darkenwald & Merriam 1982). Continuing education indicates that the adult learner is continuously pursuing education beyond the school, that is, throughout his or her life span. Colleges and universities, as well as many professional organizations, generally refer to their adult education activities as continuing education, where public school systems frequently use the term adult education.

Campbell (1977) also observed this fact. Continuing education, is often used to denote adult learning at an elevated level, including the advancement of professional or vocational competence, following initial and formal training, or it may simply mean education continued after departure from the school or any other educational institution.

Clearly, conceptualizing adult education is not an easy task. Rivera (1982) noted that this difficulty lies in the vastness and diversity of the field in its breadth of study and extent of practice. Accordingly, it means different things to different adult educators including others concerned with the education of adults.

At a conference on the theme, continuing education for the library and information science professions; Sheila (1985), attributes that continuing education is everything other than initial education, the sustained preparatory period of formal study to whatever level completed before making main employment.

Continuing education ranges from the most basic levels of study to post graduate, and provides opportunities to acquire basic skills and knowledge; a second chance to follow higher or further education courses, which people are unable or unwilling to undertake upon leaving school; opportunities to update or increase skills relating to employment in mid-career, or a means of preparing for change in lifestyle and personal circumstances, or developing latent interests and abilities.

No one, however long or comprehensive their initial education, can hope or should expect to acquire during it all the skills and knowledge they will need during a working life of perhaps 40 years. To emphasize the above point, the policy making committee of a University Grants Committee (HMSO, London.1984) in Great Britain issued a statement to the effect that, continuing education needs to be fostered not only for its essential role in promoting economic prosperity but also for its contribution to personal development and social progress. It can renew personal confidence, regenerate the human spirit, and restore a sense of purpose to people's life through the cultivation of new interests. In short, both effective economic performance and harmonious social relationships depend on our ability to deal successfully with the changes and uncertainties, which are now ever-present in our personal and working lives.

What is Continuing Education

Consumers, government agencies, and officials are demanding better service for all consumers. Concerns for professional competency and the exploding knowledge and technology in business and the workplace are cited as valid reasons contributing towards the need for continuing education. Workers and their organizations face ever- increasing rates of change in products and services, structures, procedures, processes of work, and policies and regulations intended to ensure public safety and confidence. Therefore CPE are fields of practice charged with fostering the necessary change to address these ongoing needs of the profession.

Continuing education is defined as systematic efforts to provide educational opportunities beyond formal education and initial entry into a profession (Houle, 1980). It enables practitioners to maintain competence, become aware of new developments in their field, and helps to provide responsible and quality services. Targeting professionals to keep up with current trends and issues, the practice of CPE for many years is often fueled by the regulatory requirements and professions tying continuing education to licensure, certification, or practice. They focus on particular technical and professional skills and emphasize the importance of being updated with changes in one's profession.

The continuing education system is a system submerged within a larger system. At the surface it is a component of adult education since it is concerned with the spread of general, social, vocational, and professional knowledge for all adults. It is also a subsystem of the business and service structure since the participants support or delivers products and services. This is where adult education and continuing education are subsystems of the total education system.

In traditional education, the role of the teacher is to deposit knowledge, skills, and attitudes into their students. The business and service profession usually determines what is to be taught and how it is to be taught. However, when it comes to continuing education, these professionals should be able determine their own learning, at their own pace, and on their own terms. The learning must be relevant to the profession and useful in the workplace.

Continuing education methods should reflect life-like situations. An example provided by Houle (1980), competencies must reflect life tasks of the health care professional such as diagnosing health problems, establishing priorities in care, planning and organizing health actions, and evaluating results.

Delivery strategies for continuing education programs should include informal and formal methods such as self-paced study, independent study, small groups, tutorials, problem based learning, computer-assisted instruction, and distance learning. The learning environment should include special facilities set up for education within the workplace since the most important learning environment will be the world at large where professionals live and work, not where they went to school.

There are many definitions or viewpoints on continuing professional education and it can lead to either confusion or overlapping. The researcher will try to clarify this. According to Jarvis (1995), continuing education has long been a popular idea among people concerned with the education of adults and it often comes with different names, i.e., permanent education, lifelong education, recurrent education. Jarvis further describes continuing education as a term that refers specifically to post-initial education which includes both vocational and non-vocational education. It can thus be seen as all forms of in-service training.

Houle (1980) refers to CPE as continuing learning while Cervero (1988) sees CPE as a significant area of educational activity. Jarvis (1999) cites the definition of CPE provided by the Accrediting Commission of the Continuing Education Council of the United States as "the further development of human abilities after entrance into employment or voluntary activities. It includes in-service, upgrading and updating education. Continuing education is concerned primarily with broad personal and professional development.

Knox (1986) sees continuing education as the process of systematic learning to prepare for the field of practice and to maintain proficiency in the context of constant changing knowledge base and practice. An adjunct of evolving professional careers is a continuum of preparatory and continuing education to enable practitioners to progress from novice to expert.

Houle (1980) defines CPE as the ways in which professionals try - throughout their active lives of service - to refresh their own knowledge and ability and build a sense of collective responsibility to society. This definition stretches the responsibility of the professional beyond their personal development and recognizes that professionals have a special responsibility and, by implication, a particular status in society. In order to maintain this status, the professional is required to move beyond the achievement of initial qualification to CPE.

Welsh and Woodward (1989) considered that the key issue is competence, and that it is with CPE that individual professional competence is maintained and approved. They also consider that the role of the professional bodies is not only about safeguarding standards but also about continuing competence and questions of CPE policy and practices. CPE is not a fringe activity; indeed, Todd (1987) considers it to be one of the most important resources a professional can draw on to maintain competence.

Kennie (1998) defines CPE as the systematic maintenance, improving and broadening of knowledge and the development of personal qualities necessary for the education of professional and technical duties throughout the practitioner's working life. He further emphasizes that for a professional to maintain the quality and relevance of knowledge and skill, a professional should continuously be learning throughout the practitioner's working life and professionally focus on the execution of professional and technical duties that related to maintaining the quality and relevance of professional services. Programs must be structured to include the development of personal qualities and must be conducted systematically.

CPE Concept

Houle's concept of professional education is grouped into 3 categories of competencies. They are conceptual competencies - requiring as many members of a profession to be actively involved in clarifying its function(s).

Professional competencies focus on issues such as the mastering of knowledge, skills, and attributes whereas developmental competency focuses on the futuristic development of the organization, individual and the society. Houle (1980), further defined continuing professional education as the ways in which professionals try, throughout their active lives of service, to refresh their own knowledge and ability and build a sense of collective responsibility to society.

This definition stretches the responsibility of the professional beyond their personal development and recognizes that professionals have a special responsibility and, by implication, a particular status in society. In order to maintain this status the professional is required to move beyond the achievement of the initial qualification to continuing professional education. Welsh and Woodward (1989) considered that the key issue is competence and that it is by continuing professional education that the individual professional competence is maintained and approved. They also consider that the role of the professional bodies is not only about safeguarding standards but also about continuing competence, questions of CPE policy and practices.

Houle (1980) identifies characteristics of the professionalization process, which support goals for continuing learning. They are:

Conceptual competencies to:
 i. Improve performance in the current job
 ii. Enhance career prospects
 iii. Increase learning capacity
 iv. Manage the organization.

Professional competencies:
 i. Ability to perform task required by professional duties
 ii. Technical skills and technical knowledge to interpret and solve problems
 iii. Interpersonal skills to work with and alongside others
 iv. Commercial skills to run a profitable organization

Developmental competencies focusing on:

    i.   Negotiation skills

    ii.   Counseling and monitoring skills

    iii. Communication / presentation skills

    iv. Tertiary education

    v.   Organizational development

Houle's (1980) concept of professional education that emphasizes more on the 'professional person' could help to develop a further framework on the stakeholders of continuing professional education, i.e., participants, providers, change agents, regulatory bodies, workplace leaders and developers of program for continuing professional education (Young 1998).

Furthermore, the study would also look into the collaborative effort (Cervero 1992, 1988) among providers (Davis and Botkin 1994), the investment made as a provider of continuing professional education and how much has continuing professional education integrated into the lives of professionals (Collins 1998).

The research would also investigate the issues to be negotiated in building systems of continuing education. The issues covered the question of 'what' professionals are updated with, 'how' professionals are 'updated' (Schon 1987), who benefits from continuing education (Umble and Cervero 1996), and who will provide continuing education (Cervero 1984).

The Need for CPE

Literature shows that the need for continuing professional education is crucial. According to Jarvis (1983), the needs of the educational process are about the learners rather that about the profession or wide society and the needs of continuing professional education may relate intrinsically to the needs of the profession or those of the wide society.

However as Singh and Rice (1986) points out, continuing professional education philosophy and practice should be learner centered, and accomplished in a climate wherein the profession begins to realize the value of continuing professional education and engages in this type of professional development voluntarily.

Houle (1980) identifies several objectives of continuing professional education, including clarifying the profession's functions, mastery of theoretical knowledge, self enhancement, formal training, credentialing, creation of subculture, legal reinforcement, public acceptance, ethical practice, penalties and relations to users of services. He believes that the ultimate aim of continuing professional education is to prepare practitioners not only to use the best ideas and techniques of the moment but also to expect that they will be modified or replaced.

He also believes that the primary responsibility for learning should rest with the individual and the goals of continuing professional education should be concerned with the entire process of professionalization. The continuing of professional education should be considered part of a process which continues throughout life, the patterns of methods of continuing professional education should be planned and conducted in terms of one of the three modes of education: inquiry, instruction, performance.

The provision of CPE should be expanded to pervade all aspects of professional life, professions should collaborate in planning and providing continuing professional education and the process of re-credentialing should be thoroughly rethought to determine the appropriate role of continuing professional education.

Houle (1989), emphasizes that every professional has a need to be able to carry out their duties according to the highest possible standards of character and competence and one way to meet this is to engage in a lifelong study and to achieve its greatest potential, continuing education must fulfill the promise to its name and be truly be continuing and not casual, sporadic or opportunistic. This fact means essentially that it must be self-directed and each professional must be the ultimate monitor of his or her own learning, controlling the stable or shifting design of its continuity.

Houle further argues that continuing education must be based not only on content oriented goals of keeping up with the new development; it must also be designed to facilitate changes in life patterns or career lines. Accordingly, Fryer (1997) states that learning at the workplace will need to accommodate the needs and interests of a variety of stakeholders, including employees, employers, customers, government and providers. It will contribute to competitiveness, skills enhancement, employability and capacity to deal with change.

This supports the view that the culture of lifelong learning forms the foundation for new models facing radical changes at the workplace. The reasons being, new knowledge is being required at a greater rate than ever before, so that knowledge gained only a short while ago becomes obsolete and advances in technology are accelerating at a rate unimagined ten years ago, and the workforce has to change constantly to keep up to date.

The dynamic and rapidly changing human resource, training, education, real estate agency and other fields demand lifelong learning. Some of the reasons are as follows:

    i.   To maintain competence among professional practitioners.

    ii. To avoid professional obsolescence.

Factors, which contribute to professional obsolescence, are as follows:

    i.   Decreasing inclination with age to do professional reading, to attend educational programs, and to maintain professional membership;

    ii. Failure to perceive the past, present, and future changes in knowledge affecting practice;

    iii. Absence of desire for a broader education through self-directed or formally organized learning experiences;

    iv. Lack of personal initiative to continue learning in any format; and desire to maintain the status quo.

Maintenance of competency is the responsibility of the individual. A true professional realizes that continuous learning is essential to a lifetime of service to the public. Continuing education implies a system of life-long learning, personal self-development, and actualization of needs. Continuing education is created out of a demand realized by the individual as a desire to upgrade one's skill and competence. Continuing education is many things to many people. It is a route to professional advancement, a means to an increase in salary, or fulfillment of the desire to perform as effectively as possible. It can also be a burdensome requirement to some.

Disadvantages to Mandatory Continuing Education

There are discussions whether professional bodies should make CPE mandatory, as programs should originate from them as described by Mattran (1981). As argued by him, can CPE make all professionals who participated in the CPE program competent. For example, whether they are from the medical, engineering, real estate or accounting group. Participants after the program have showed concern that the program providers, have not provided them with a choice in developing the curriculum as well as choosing the facilitator. As such continuing education workshops have fallen out as it did not meet the candidates' needs. On the other hand participants sometimes rush just to obtain CPE points to renew their license to practice. As argued by Rockhill (1981) restricts individual freedom to choose as well as, has negative effects for adult education and does not meet the desired requirement.

Professionals owe the public certain standards and profiency in updating themselves with new knowledge and skills which is available from time to time. As such Darkenwald & Merriam (1982) echoed this point in supporting that, professional bodies should not protect incompetent practitioners' or for that matter not conductingmandatory CPE. They suggested progressive evaluation on their performance and deny re-licensure to those who fail to demonstrate continued proficiency. In this context Houle (1980) observed that knowledge and skill learnt is not enough to update proficiency but to practice it will keep the skill going. CPE workshops' may partially contribute to competence but practitioners' may lack resources at their workplace, like; equipments, machines, technology upgrade, or policy and regulation change. At the same time, as argued by Rockhill (1981) regulation governing professional competence may change which has little to do with updates.

Cross (1981), Knowles (1984,), and Brookfield (1984) argues that, when adults are forced to learn against their own inclinations and desires, the resulting resentment is likely to become a major block to any kind of meaningful learning. Consequently, participation in compulsory continuing professional education might lead to increased statistics of adult participation but be characterized by mental absenteeism. Having said this, they concur, that mandatory CPE should be made affordable to all practitioners so as to maintain their licenses and competence

Advantages to Mandatory Continuing Education

Arguments in support of current mandatory continuing education are based on the assumption that professionals need to continue their education in order to be competent. Professional practice will be in jeopardy if professionals fail to remain current. CPE may increase their competence and knowledge and skill of the latest updates and this in-turn will result in improved performance among the professionals across any industry

Houle (1980) asserts that it is the inherent responsibility of all professionals to remain current and Cross (1981) believes that even though voluntary education is preferable, required learning is better than none. Mattran (1981) points out that professionals choosing their profession should under go mandatory as required by their professional bodies governing them. This is also to oversee that public has laid trust over them to practice professionally and in trust, as such CPE should not be seen as an infringement but to abide to the law and standards set, Professional bodies, themselves are dynamic in nature as such, members practicing should be dynamic in nature too.

Currently, the mandate and requirements for continuing education are coming from professional groups. This is appropriate as it does not violate these requirements and many professional groups, prefer periodic examinations to continuing education. Most professionals enjoy and receive several benefits from participating in continuing education programs.

In a study based on a needs assessment of continuing real estate professional education, it was found that 81 percent of realtors' surveyed said that continuing education was important to them professionally. These offers can stimulate and enhance the abilities of real estate professionals. CPE courses provide an opportunity to get away from normal routines and be exposed to new ideas. They can also help prevent burnout and allow networking with professional colleagues.

To make mandatory continuing education more enhancing to the professional practitioners', Rockhill (1981) suggest that professional providers' make the workshop appealing. The program design must be current, facilitator should be dynamic, and cost must be competitive in nature. Further, under current requirements, professionals have an extremely wide range of educational alternatives. They can select workshops from a large listing of continuing education programs and to some extent even home study is available. Therefore, professionals can meet requirements with very little effort, since there is so much of variety and flexibility, they can also choose courses that are most stimulating to them with educational settings that best fit their individual preferences.

CPE programs, as concluded by Mattran (1981), can also serve as a catalyst for more formal programs. For example, programs sponsored by Boston University School of Social Work sparked such interest that they led to a part-time M.S.W. graduate satellite program. Also, the Family Beginnings program, offered by St. Anne's Hospital in Fall River, Massachusetts was met with such enthusiasm by social workers and hospital pediatricians that it paved the way for discussions of a pediatric mental health residency program.

Furthermore the issue of mandatory versus voluntary continuing education is controversial. Many believe that being a professional implies commitment to lifelong learning to pursue practice-enhancing skills, therefore continuing education need not be mandated (Glacken, 1981). Due to advances in knowledge and technology and the public demand for accountability and consumer protection, the number of states mandating continuing education for professionals has significantly increased in the last 10 years. Those opposed to mandatory continuing education argue it violates adult learning principles, which include voluntary participation, informal education, self-direction, and attention to individual learning needs.

Professionals are supposed to be autonomous, self-managed, and responsible for mastery of knowledge. Mandatory continuing education is punitive to those who voluntarily participate. Evidence that continuing education results in improved practice or competency is lacking. Programs are not consistently and uniformly available. Many lack quality and relevance to practitioner needs and encourage providers of continuing education programs to focus on profit. Requiring participation may hinder learning by reducing motivation and individual responsibility. Some argue professionals should be accountable for effective performance, not participation.

Glacken (1981) argues out these questions; every profession has lazy or uncaring people who do not keep up with their field. Mandatory continuing education will force them to stay current and placing the onus on these patterns and questions:

- Lazy people make up the majority or minority of practitioners;
- Mandatory CE disrupts a person's learning style;
- Most CE is given in a lecture format. Is this compatible with everyone's learning style?
- Independent study and experiential learning are not usually acceptable forms of CE.
- Forcing participation can be time consuming and/or unrealistic especially when CE programs are inaccessible, expensive, and require travel to distant locations.

With increased knowledge, professionals will be more competent and caring.
- Research does not substantiate this claim.
- Attendance does not insure learning has occurred.
- Knowing facts does not perfect skills.
- Competency does not increase compassion or improve attitudes.
- Affective (attitudinal) domain is rarely addressed in CE.

Someone else knows better than a professional what should be learned and how it should be learned. This questions the concept of professionalism since being a professional means keeping current and maintaining competency. True professionals realize continuous learning is essential to a lifetime of service to the public and forced participation frustrates competent professionals since they feel the public does not trust their competency or their ability to maintain that competency. Public believes mandatory CE will screen out incompetent practitioners to ensure the right people are in place.

The proponents of mandatory continuing education believe to expect individuals to voluntarily participate in continuing education is unrealistic. Mandates are necessary to protect the public from incompetent practitioners. Some evidence exists that well-designed programs can influence effective practice. Although imperfect, continuing education programs are better than examinations or practice reviews.

Continuing Professional Education Unit (CPEU)

The continuing professional education unit (CPEU) is the system of measuring continuing education in terms of the extent of participation. One CPEU is defined as ten contact hours of participation in an organized continuing education experience under responsible sponsorship, capable direction, and qualified instruction (Kerka, 1994). The CPEU concept was developed during the late 1960's to establish a method or recording participation that would provide credits for courses at institutions of higher learning.

The CPEU was designed to be easily measurable, flexible as to method, transferable from one record keeping system to another (standardized), able to meet content requirements of degrees and certificates, and usable as a metering device for measuring teaching load. Although used by many professional organizations, the CPEU has never gained full acceptance.

Some reasons cited are that CPEU's are not capable of being standardized, there is no strong accrediting body that oversees CPEU's, and CPEU earnings do not assure changes in competence of performance.

CHAPTER 4

CPE AND PROGRAM DEVELOPMENT

Program Development Framework

Cervero (1988) presents and articulates the approaches of program development strategies for professional's continuing education and discusses the planning framework used by continuing educators. The question of which planning framework is effective is compared through theories developed by Nowlen (1988), Sork and Busky (1986), Apps (1985), Houle (1980) and Pennington and Green (1976). Cervero (1988) argues that the continuing educator or change-agent influences planning framework. Furthermore, different institutions offer different opportunities or constraints impinging on the continuing educators 'theory-in-use' about developing programs.

Program development framework is usually based on textbook material. These frameworks are difficult to 'use' because continuing educators come with a set of believe strongly entrenched in them. They are influenced by the environment, system, political factors, and budgetary constraints that constantly alter neatly, conceived plans of action(Brookfield 1986).Every planner of a continuing education program must remain in control of whatever process, principle, or pattern they find useful (Houle 1980).

Sork and Busky (1986) defined a program development framework as, 'a set of steps, tasks, or decisions which, when carried out, produce the design and outcome specifications for a systematic instructional activity'.

The definition of a program is the product resulting from all the program activities in which the professional educator and learner are involved. This would include need analysis planning, instruction, promotion, evaluation and reporting.

On the same note, program development is also defined as a deliberate series of actions and decisions through which representatives of the people affected by the potential program are involved with a programmer to:

i. Develop an organizational structure for analyzing, interpreting and making decisions for planned change
ii. Effective use of resources
iii. Establish priorities
iv. Identify desired outcomes
v. Identify resources and support staff to implement the program
vi. Design an instructional plan
vii. Implement a plan of action
viii. Develop appropriate accountability with regards to the effectiveness of the value of the program
ix. Communicate the value of the program to the stakeholders.

Program planning is a complex process. There are however a variety of models that organizes the process according to a series of sequential and/or overlapping steps or stages. Various adult educators (Knox, 1986; Griffin, 1993; Caffarella, 1994) advocate a participatory approach in planning educational or training programs.

Program planning (Boyle 1982) is the product resulting from the programming activities in which the professional educator and learner are involved. This will include need analysis, planning, institution, promotion, evaluation and reporting. Prior to considering a specific program model, Caffarella (1994), stresses that the planner should examine their belief to determine whether the planning model they intend to use will fit with who they are and how they prefer to practice instructional processes with.

Practitioners should remember that one of the basic assumptions of the model is that collaborative planning is given in most planning situations. According to Brookfield (1986), years of experience dealing with organizations in which personality conflicts, political factors and budgetary constraints constantly alter neatly conceived plans of actions. This should not come as a surprise as the little research done suggests that virtually no continuing educators use these planning frameworks, even for programs that are successful.

Most continuing educators operate out of their own planning framework, which is influenced by their own personal values and beliefs and the institutional context in which they work. The central task for effective practice is to make one's own framework explicit, analyze its assumptions and principles, and alter it when necessary. If continuing professional educators are to become reflective practitioners (Schon, 1983), they must constantly be engaged in this important task.

Program Development

Program development is therefore defined as a deliberate service of actions and decisions through which both the learner and programmer are involved in realizing their mutual outcome. Continuing educators have been planning programs for groups of professionals for decades. These educators have tended to use systematic processes in their planning.

In the past, some of these systematic processes have been codified as planning frameworks to provide guidance to others working in the field. Sork and Busky (1986) define a program development framework in a way that is appropriate for this study; it is a set of steps, tasks or decisions which, when carried out, produce the design and outcome specifications for a systematic instructional activity.

The pioneer in planning frameworks can be traced to Tyler's (1949) influential book on "Basic Principles of Curriculum Instruction". Tyler suggested that any curriculum development process should be guided by four questions:
  i.   What educational experiences should the school seek to attain?
  ii. What educational experiences can be provided that is likely to attain these purposes?
  iii. How can these educational purposes be effectively organized?
  iv. How can we determine whether these purposes are being attained?

Apps (1985) notes that these four questions can be translated into five tasks common to most program development frameworks: identifying learners needs, defining objectives, identifying learning experiences that meet these objectives, organizing learning experiences into an educational plan and evaluating the outcomes of the educational effort in accordance with the objectives.

A study by Pennington and Green (1976) interviewed fifty-two continuing professional educators of higher institutions and asked them to report on the planning processes they used in a recent successful program. In comparing these planning processes with ideal frameworks described in the literature, they found major discrepancies.

Firstly, little comprehensive needs assessment was done due to a lack of time, expertise or resources. The planners provided lip service to the importance of needs assessment, very few followed through. Secondly, objectives were not stated as to what the learner will learn from the program; and thirdly, there were no indication that the design of instruction was based on learner characteristics, desired learning outcomes, time, money or other available resources. Lastly, comprehensive evaluation was not done. To this effect, the authors concluded that the way planners describe their actions are 'that personal values, environment constraints, available resources and other factors impinge on the program development process'.

Houle (1980) suggests that this should not be taken as negative, as it means that planners are responding to the situation in which they work. Houle (1980) also suggests that every planner of a continuing education program must remain in control of whatever process, principle, or pattern they find useful. To this effect, effective practice is based on being able to fully understand one's own planning framework, know how to evaluate it, and be able to change it when necessary.

Sork (1983) found that out of twenty-two reports dealing with program development in continuing professional education, ten are books and the rest are articles on planning frameworks. When he compared the planning frameworks on six different dimensions, three relates to characteristics of the planning milieu in which they were designed to be used and differ in the level of program emphasized and the client orientation system. The other three are evaluative dimensions that differentiate the frameworks based on features that might limit or enhance their utility for specific users.

Most planning frameworks are designed for potential participants who are members of a single formal organization, such as a professional association or employing agency, and the emphasis is on 'how' rather than 'why' of program development. Argyris and Schon (1974) argue that professionals must develop their own continuing theory of practice under real time conditions. Continuing educators should understand their own theories in use about developing programs and use them as effectively as possible.

These are some of the contextual factors that affect theory-in-use. Continuing professional education as a field of practice would become more effective if program developers began to see themselves as practical theorists (Brookfield, 1986). They can do this by analyzing their own practice and peeling back the layers of words that sometimes obscure the meaning of what they do(Apps, 1985). By doing so explicitly and disseminating to others their theories-in-use, program developers could present actual planning frameworks as alternatives to the prescriptive frameworks, which dominate currently.

Planning is the sub-process of the whole programming process. The following are the key words linked with programming: purposive method, scheme of arrangement, design, devise, liberate and rational activities. General planning is the process whereby the planner and the receivers of the program devise together how they will carry out a learning process together. Planning involves more than just coming with a blue print of what the planner and the receivers are going to do but also the element of commitment to helping one another to better understand the content as well as a person.

Purpose of Planning

In program planning, we begin by looking at what is the purpose of the educational program. Educational programs sometimes serve more than one purpose. Educational program for adults are conducted for five primary purposes for a variety of audiences as illustrated in the following examples (Pennington and Green, 1976; Apps, 1985): to encourage continuous growth and development of an individual, to assist people in responding to practical problems and issues of adult life, to prepare people for current and future work opportunities, to assist organizations in achieving desired results and adapting to change, to provide opportunities and to examine community and social issues.

A program needs to be adequately planned because planning helps us to have road maps of what we are going to do. A program also helps us to achieve better targets. By planning programs, we have a better control of the programs; enhance the evaluation process so that when something goes wrong, steps can be taken to correct it. Planning gives meaning and system to the action to be taken and prepares the basis for a course of future actions.

Expectations of a Program

The expectation of change is an outcome or result of the educational program. Educational programs foster three kinds of change:

  i.   Individual change related to the acquisition of new knowledge, building of skills and examination of personal values and beliefs.
  ii. Organizational change resulting in new or revised policies, procedures and ways of working.
  iii. Community and social change that allows for differing segments of society to respond to the world around them in alternative ways.

How Are Educational Programs Planned

Some educational programs are carefully planned while others are literally thrown together. Careful planning of educational programs does not guarantee their success. Careful planning will be able to provide the guide or roadmap to assist them from the start to the finish of any program.

Good planning requires the ability to synthesize facts and value judgments in process of sound decision-making about the objectives the program should attain and what courses of action are most likely to achieve them.

The ability to plan requires: an understanding of nature and function of planning, skill in formulating planning procedures, skill in identifying problems and needs, skill in formulating means and wise courses of action to attain objectives and, skill in involving key leaders in the planning process (Knox, 1986).

Planners who are primarily responsible for the design of professional education programs have special concerns. Nowlen (1988) describes two potential yet distinct planning models for membership and staff development: the competency based model and the performance or up-to-date model. Each model has its own advantages and disadvantages.

The competency-based model specifically addresses needs, knowledge or skills required by professionals to enhance whatever they do for a living. One limitation to the competency-based model is its restriction to the prescriptive definitions of what the professional ought to be, although these may be difficult to clarify. The performance or up-to-date model is characterized as being adaptive to changing needs and as having a broader purpose or perspective.

Nowlen (1988) states that the performance model's field of vision is alert to signs that a professional's knowledge and skills need to be refreshed or updated, and that new research, technology and societal developments need to be brought instructively to a professional's attention. The up-to-date model highlights the importance of remaining current with new research and new technology. Each of these concerns also affects the professional's career and advancement possibilities. The performance model draws attention to the situations, which the professional may face in his / her career.

Nowlen supports the use of performance model and concludes that the professional's success or failure may be interwoven with his or her ability to adapt, live, work and find meaning within the diverse culture of various settings. Edelson (1992) claims that program planning cannot exist as though the process operates in a vacuum. He proposes a systems approach and suggests that program planning must be linked to larger external organizational and contextual issues, including working within a framework of continuing educational policy.

Edelson expounds that adults and continuing education leaders should take existing policy as a point of departure for developing their own policies and action plans. These plans must be reexamined and deconstructed to determine their meanings and to see if they are still valid guides. As well, Edelson suggests that education leaders employ advisory committees as a method to commence effective program planning. Advisory committees may consist of staff as well as other organizational members. While advisory committees may create organizational conflict, the systems approach is an effective process, which can be used to gain new insights into the planning process and can prevent programs from becoming stagnant.

Richey (1992) proposes a systemic training model, which identifies factors in need of training intervention. Richey's model includes three components: conceptual factors which affect adult learning, a procedural guide to design practice, and a theory component consisting of propositions which both describe the learning process and prescribe the design process. This planning framework incorporates four variables: the learner, the content, the environment, and the delivery of instruction.

Richey concludes that there is considerable research evidence to warrant a belief that these factors affect learning outcomes directly or indirectly by interacting with other elements of the model. One advantage to Richey's model is that it provides for simultaneous consideration of a variety of factors, which influence learning, and hence influences the program planning and design process.

Korten (1980) discusses the textbook model for program planning. He refers to the design as the blueprint model because of its emphasis on pre-planning processes. Korten states researchers are supposed to provide data that will allow the planners to choose the most cost effective project design for achieving a given development outcome and to reduce it to a blueprint for implementation.

Administrators, managers and others who are responsible for implementation execute the plan according to the specific intentions of the blueprint. When using this model, Korten stresses that the plans are expected to be carried out as stipulated in the original blueprint plan. He notes that at the evaluation stage, if changes are identified, the blueprint is revised. Korten points out that the blueprint-planning model has its advantages. It provides planners with a sense of order and it can identify easily defensible budget presentations. A program planner must evaluate his or her own situation as well as the learning situation itself before making a fixed determination on which planning model is advantageous. Some planning models may be more time consuming than others; the planner will have to evaluate which model suits his or her needs depending on the particular programming situation.

Participatory Approaches in Programming

The design of training programs should not occur in isolation from program participants. For example, the design of programs intended for people living in underdeveloped countries, under extremely impoverished circumstances, or otherwise where basic instructional materials are not available will be very different from the design of programs intended for people with access to better facilities and resources.

Kenny (1985) explores the differences in planning education for disadvantaged students living under an oppressive regime versus planning for middle and upper class students in an affluent society. He describes society is characterized by a structure of dominance, what should be the nature of the education of those at the middle and top of society, but more precisely what sort of education for those students would help to end the structure of dominance.

In attempting to answer his own question, Kenny relies on arguments developed by Freire (1970), who maintains that people should be helped to see their own situation in their own terms, through posing problems of their relationship to the world in the framework of a critical dialogue conducted within small discussion groups and the results can lead to action toward liberation from the structure of dominance. Freire strongly advocates participatory education among those who live under domineering regimes.

Participatory approaches for planning new programs are more widely used than ever before. Advanced capitalist societies traditionally characterized by a high degree of technology also have a demand today for participatory planning of new programs. This approach is especially evident in planning programs for unemployed people brought on, in part, by the growth of information technology. Mott and Daley (2000) state that participants should have input into the design of the program.

As programs are often designed before all participants are selected, perhaps the administrator should ensure that representative participants have genuine input into the design of the program. This recommendation is related to recruitment and access to information about the participants. Apps (1989) believes that a broad spectrum of people should be involved in the planning process and those who are involved in the planning of educational programs, including professionals, educators, and bureaucrats, need to see themselves as being involved in the learning process along with others.

One of the implications of sharing in the responsibility of the program planning process is that it lends relevance to the learner for what he intends to learn. Supporting this, McClean (1996) says that the formative stages of the program planning process require the conducting of a needs assessment. He suggests that the needs assessment process should shift from concentrating on questions about what the educator expects to teach to questions that allow the learners to express what they believe they need. Benson (2001) maintains that the design of the program should be custom-made depending on the complexity of the skill taught. The instructor therefore must decide the best teaching method to deliver the subject material to a particular group of people.

He states that a variety of approaches can be used, including computer-assisted instruction, learner-provided and learner generated materials, and cooperative learning exercises. Askov also emphasizes the need for a comprehensive evaluation process to be included in the curriculum design and all stakeholders must be involved in the curriculum design, on-going evaluation with all shareholders having an opportunity to suggest indicators of success for which can help shape curriculum development to make it appropriate and responsive to the needs of all involved.

Benson believes that adult educators responsible for the design of programs should not attempt in isolation. Boone (1985) emphasizes the importance of a training program being linked to the participants' specific needs and requirements. As he sees it, a collaborative approach to program planning should be adopted between the adult educators and the participants.

Similarly, the importance of collaboration was noted by Mitroff (1983) who states that programs started without consultation by the government or other organizations, - if not related to people's needs- soon fail, however big the initial fanfare. This is a lesson which every practical-minded planner and social worker cannot afford to forget. In brief, the planning approach should reflect the learner's socio, economic, political, legal and cultural backgrounds, ensuring that these specific variables have been met. This requirement is especially true in a training context.

As Boone (1985) states, an adult educator's decision with regard to specific programming strategies should be based on the particular cultural group at which the program may be directed. The socio-cultural and political factors affecting the planning process cannot be ignored.

Planning Models

Program planning models consists of ideas of one or more persons about how a program should be put together and what ingredients are necessary to ensure successful outcomes. These models come in all shapes and sizes. They could range from a simple orientation to a complex and comprehensive one.

A program-planning model is usually conceived as an "open" or "closed" system. In a closed system, all inputs to the system can be identified and meeting the outcomes can be both predetermined and ensured.

An open system recognizes outside factors, which are out of the planner's control. Simple to complex happenings can affect both the substance and the outcomes of planned program. Some planning models are linear. The planner is expected to start at step one and follow each step in sequential order until the process is completed. Some planning models are processes that consist of a set of interacting and dynamic elements and components and decision points.

Boone (1985) presents a planning model that includes four basic steps:
- Assessing clients' needs
- Setting objectives, and acquiring instructional resources

- Ensuring participation in learning activities
- Conducting a program evaluation.

Although Boone lists these steps sequentially, he notes that they also possess an overlapping quality. Even though each step requires specific action, planners often must deal with more than one step at a time. They need time to consider future and past steps within the context of the current step, and within the whole planning and design process. On the other hand, prior to considering a specific program model, Caffarella (1994) stresses that the planner should examine his or her own beliefs to determine whether the planning model they intend to use will fit with who they are and how they prefer to practice instructional processes. Assuming the planners is to work alone then, the interactive program-planning model will not work for them, as the model is based on a collaborative planning mode.

Planners should use a stakeholder-based planning model by taking into account the needs and interests of the internal and external stakeholders, or people who significantly affect or are affected by the program (Mitroff, 1983). When they do the program is likely to be implemented well, achieve its objectives, and garner enough support to be sustained. Planners must be also be able to breach the relevant stakeholder groups and how they relate to and depend on one another; understand their interests in relation to the program; build a planning and implementation process that takes their situation, needs and interests into account; and evaluate all their program's processes and effects to see how the groups are being served and what can be improved (Cervero & Wilson, 1994; Umble, Cervero, & Langone, 2001). Planners also need several strategies of negotiation to enact these frameworks effectively.

The Interactive Model

The interactive program-planning model for adults draws many ideas from previous proposed models of program planning which include those described by Houle (1972), Knowles (1980), Sork and Caffarella (1989) and Tracey (1992). The difference between these models lie in the combination and comprehensiveness of the components and tasks that are included, the suggested ways the model can be used by practitioners and its focus on practical ideas for making decisions and completing program planning tasks for each components of the model. The interactive program-planning model is derived from classical and current description of program planning, principles and practices of adult learning, and practical experience.

This planning model, among many other models, is not a step by step but rather a program in which planners work with a number of planning components and tasks at the same time and not necessarily in any particular order. Most programs for adult learners are produced by people with multiple interests, working in specific institutional context that profoundly affect their content and form (Cervero and Wilson, 1992). The program planner can start and end the planning process at any particular place. There is no one place to start or to end the planning process. The key to using this model of program planning is flexibility.

Caffarella (1994) states eleven components of the interactive model:
  i.   Establishing a basis for the planning process.
  ii. Identifying program ideas.
  iii. Sorting and prioritizing program ideas.
  iv. Develop program objectives.
  v.   Preparing for the transfer of learning.
  vi. Formulating evaluation plans.
  vii. Determining formats, schedules and staff needs.
  viii.Preparing budgets and marketing plans.
  ix. Designing instructional plans.
  x.   Coordinating facilities and on-site events.
  xi. Communicating the value of the program.

The above model is grounded on six major assumptions drawn primarily from Houle (1972), Knowles (1980), Sork and Caffarella (1989), and Cervero and Wilson (1992, 1994). Among these assumptions, two are critical for those using the interactive model:
  i.   The program should focus on what the participants actually learn and how this learning results in changes in the participants, organizations and societal issues.
  ii. The development of educational programs is a complete interaction of institutional priorities, tasks, people and events.

CPE Models

Nowlen (1988) described three models of continuing professional education, all of which can be beneficial models from a range of perspectives. The Update Model, Competence Model and Performance Model are three approaches to developing continuing education for professionals. A brief description of the strengths and weaknesses of each model is discussed within this chapter.

The Update Model

The central characteristic of the update model is rich in information and didactic short courses. It employs a variety of instructional methods and techniques. The update model updates professionals in their practice through 'knowledge update' and 'information update' but these updates are not guaranteed to improve competency, proficiency or performance. When asked by professionals, what is the structure of the field, Nowlen and Houle (1988, p.77) asserts that

> "At minimum, continuing professional education appears to be complexes of instructional systems, many of them heavily didactic, in which people who know something teach to those who do not know it. The central aim of such teaching offered by many providers is to keep professionals up to date in their practice. But the achievement of this goal is usually evaluated indirectly, chiefly by counting the number of people involved in an activity or assessing their attitude toward it."

The above quote accurately captures the argument. In this context the field of the instructional systems is quite varied. The tools being teleconferencing, decision trees, interactive computer terminals, videotaped case studies and simulations executive games are adaptive to the field, and stimulated instructions often lead to objective evaluation.

The update model is widely used in continuous professional education and is extremely popular among professionals. While it cannot be disputed that the participants might return from such programs highly enlightened, it generally does not improve the competence and performance of the participants. Schon

(1983) demonstrates in 'the reflective practitioner' these positivists construct places basic science, including related skills and attitudes and problem solving.

This model is also dominant of professional practice. Professionals often say that they feel most professional when they are applying a research based technique or protocol, when their problem solving is firmly grounded in the world of certainty, stability and rigor. As these short courses are highly didactic, the participants are seldom tested or evaluated for their competence. It does however create an illusion on the part of the participants that he has participated in continuing professional education, has increased competence and has met whatever requirements of the organization or profession with respect to continuous education.

On the other hand, it is worthwhile to note that, as stated by Nowlen (1988) most people in business and the professions cope everyday with uncertainty, indeterminate, complex, unique and unstable circumstances. They do demonstrate art, craft and wisdom. They are often at a loss to explain how they do it and have difficulty showing others how to do it. Some of the weakness of this model is that it emphasis on problem solving rather than problem definition. The value of extraordinary knowledge and experiences of professionals is directly related to problem definition because the definition of the problem is full of uncertainty, uniqueness, and conflict dimensions.

This model serves each profession separately through its individual knowledge base. It means separate approaches are required with each profession without attention to common needs and common relations of professions. At the same time being up-to-date does not guarantee the patients, clients or customers will be better off. We should not forget that the main reason for CPE is to provide higher levels of services for society. The update model rarely addresses competence related aptitudes and strengths such as interpersonal skill and motivation or personal weakness that impair competence.

The strength of this model, according to Nasseh (1999), provides practicing professionals with a level of knowledge comparable to those professionals graduating from professional schools. It closes the need gap created by changes in technology, science and skills between these two generations of professionals. In the first 60 years of this century, professional schools curricula were matrices reflecting few knowledge and skill specialties and few generic settings of practice (Nowlen, 1988). Nowlen's description of specialties is an indication of the effectiveness of the update model for that period of time.

The Competence Model

The central characteristics of the competence model are based on the ability to meet the specific requirements of the job. Competency has been defined in different ways skills, attitude, roles, traits, self-schema and motive. It is extremely popular among professional bodies like the American Society Training and Development (ASTD), American Management Academy (AMA) and the Institute of Personnel Development (IPD), UK. Competence must be properly understood and defined in precise terms before they can be useful. Competence should not be just limited to knowledge, skills, and attitudes but should be stretched to include the personality traits.

In this model, a practice audit or job function analysis becomes the basis of an assessment to a professional's educational needs. The competency-based curriculum is designed to provide required competency for professionals in order to continue practice. Competence is the quality or state of having sufficient knowledge, judgment and skill to carry out responsibility and provide desired services, or as Cyrs (1978) said, competence is a measure of both capacity to perform and performance itself. Unfortunately, competencies are generally stated in very broad terms for it to be useful, i.e. for the competencies to be evaluated against performance. It is accepted that a certified employee with the necessary competencies would be able to do the job. However, jobs when broken into its tasks and re-categorized would entail many competencies. This is a rather tedious process and unless carried through, would render the competence model useless.

To be competent is to possess sufficient knowledge and the ability to meet specified requirements in the sense of being able, adequate, suitable and capable (Cyrs, 1978) and to adopt the definition of Hall and Jones (1976), that competence is acquired intellectual, attitudinal and / or motor capabilities derived from a specified role and setting and stated in terms of performance as a broad composite or domain of behavior and which is in effect an integration or synthesis of behavioral objectives as well as some elements of covert behavior.

By changing in context of practices, generation of new practices and transformation of some professions, many efforts in the professional environment have begun to focus on competence. Employers, professional associations, and providers have all taken a serious interest in developing standards, evaluation, certification and recertification, licensure and re-licensure, and planning for long-term continuing education and reevaluation of professional school curricula.

The competence model represents the second generation of continuing professional education in the 1980s. This model has been a creative response to increasingly complex challenges faced by professionals.

Like all models, this model has their strengths and weaknesses. Some of the weaknesses are is that with this model, the assumption is that performance is entirely an individual affair that leads the model logically. Even in models that are sensitive to organizational context of professional activity, it is individual competency that is at the center of inquiry.

The competency model fails to identify competence in personal affairs as job related, and yet absence of knowledge, skill and maturity in managing private lives. A serious flaw in this model is related to the lack of addressing weakness, demerit and impairment in practice by competence model research. Lastly, this model does not include relationship of individuals with others in organizational settings, ensemble of peers, subordinates, supervisors and culture.

The strength of this model is that it does not assume the prescriptions of professional education are descriptions of practice any more. It assumes that continuing education needs of practitioners are extensions of lines of inquiry pursued in professional school. The model deals with contexts of practice both with changes and multiplied. It also evaluates professions that have undergone transformation.

The competence of professionals to provide new ways of service was the main objective of this model, which was missing from the previous model. The model introduced practice audit and job function analysis; this was a strong reason for continuing professional education for professions. Lastly, it calls not only for updates in professional school basic knowledge and skills, but also for education derived from pluralistic sources found useful is assuming competence required by what professionals actually do for a living (Cervero, Azzaretto, 1988).

One of the examples provided by Nasseh (1999) is on the use of competence model is shown by Digital Equipment Corporation, offering a seven-day intensive hands-on training class for expert system developers using forward chaining design methodology. This class will teach OPS5 programming language. University Computing Services has accepted to develop a surgical expert system for School of Nursing. UCS will send a programmer, analyst or academic application designer to this class. This is an effective way of learning a new competency for solving an existing and specific problem.

Measurement of validity of curriculum in the competence model is based on the new competency of participants in the work place. In this case, the successful contribution of an application developer in the development of an expert system has a direct relation with the quality of those seven-day training sessions.

This practice-audit model stressed small groups, collegial atmosphere, peer interaction; opportunity for informal feedback and particularly a performance orientation has been identified as a paradigm for future programs. This approach is also relatively more costly than the knowledge oriented program model (Toombs and Lindsay, 1985).

The Performance Model

Performance is the function of the individual, which is controlled by the social environment and personal factors. There are also various factors influencing performance. For example, baseline knowledge and skills, the challenge of new roles, prerequisite skills in human relations, critical skills of mind, proficiency in self managed learning, individual development progress, organizational developmental balance and fit of individual and organization to one another, skills in coping with life's surprises as well as its anticipated transitions, and the understanding of the influences of environments and cultures and the skills to orchestrate them.

A learning agenda towards meeting performance is done through competence assessment using various approaches like self-assessment instruments, national or organizational competence profiles, critical incidences interview, simulations, etc. The learning agenda can be composed of a variety of approaches, e.g. self-directed learning, mentoring, counseling, formal educational programs and assignments, etc.

As Schon (1983)equips that very little of the topography of professional practice is high, hard ground where a problem can be smoothly mapped on a decision tree. They cope everyday with uncertainty to determine, complex, unique and unstable circumstances.

The performance model focuses on all variables which have demonstrated to have a strong influence on professionals' performance; influences of environment and culture on practice, life skills, update needs, personal and organizational development balance, individual and organizational learning skill, critical skills of mind, applied human relations and new roles preparation. In addition to influences of continuing professional education in performance, there are other factors such as organizational setting, society of peers, subordinates, supervisors and individual's culture, which can play main roles in the performance.

The performance model is often given lip service by organizations. With rapid change, employees need to do a task; job or project, in half the time allowed for and use probably half the normal resources. Thus, the performance model for CPE is inevitable. This model allows for the identification of a suitable approach to obtain the required performance from an employee, and calls for a structured detail analysis of an individual's abilities and disabilities. The performance model involves a lot of work, determination and support.

As suggested by Nowlen (1988), serious research work and design is needed for bringing performance and continuing education into an organization. The initial approach should be to start with some of the factors that influence performance. For example, baseline knowledge and skills, the challenge of new roles, prerequisite skills in human relations, critical skills of mind and proficiency in self-managed learning are all needed in order to perform better. This does not involve the other factors in the performance model like individual developmental progress, organizational development, talents, the fitting of individual and organization from one to another, skills in coping with life's surprises as well as its anticipated transitions and understanding of the influences of environments and cultures and skills to orchestrate them.

As with the other models, the performance model too, has its strength and weakness. The weakness of this model has created all expectations for the ultimate performance of professions without covering details and standard procedures for accomplishment of these goals. The model has made expectations of new roles for continuing education for professions. These roles are additional and not replacement roles, but providers, institutions, professional associations and educators are not moving in the same direction; furthermore the model is too complex and costly to implement. Finally, the model needs great collaboration from different parties, even within the same organization.

As for the strength of using this model, it enables professionals to review and understand all the factors, which can have a major influence on their performance. The model sees performance as an interactive phenomenon involving more than one professional and often involving several specialties and occupations as well as clients. The model also enables continuing educators to help individual professionals by reviewing all major influences on their performance. The model introduced performance, as a function of both the individual and assemblies and it is the result of the interaction of social and personal influences. It also recognized that being a professional is an unceasing movement toward a new level of performance.

As Houle and Schon (1983)explain, that when new levels of performance are achieved, they seem inadequate because better levels of possible performance come into view. Very simply, the professionals, the environment, and the clients' expectations are evolving and changing. The teacher who entered a higher education institute 20 years ago is not the same person today. The practice of teaching and learning today is significantly different from what it was before. Constant changes bring the necessity of being life –long learners for professionals. Design of a performance model is very difficult and expensive.

It also requires major support and time commitment by organizations, professional associations, clients, peers, and continuing education providers.

Professionals and providers of CPE will have to choose a model; be it the update model, competence model, or the performance model, which suits them well and provides a holistic view of professional performance. CPE updates and competence related to job function is expected. However, the addition of new areas of expertise in professions and societies and things from professions has brought additional variables to the existing one.

CPE Practices of Professional Providers

The professional providers charged with protecting and enhancing the profession, play a major role and sometimes a controversial role in the new concern with ways of maintaining and increasing the competency of the practitioner. External pressures from consumers, governmental regulating bodies, and practitioners themselves are forcing many professional providers to conduct updates, whether it is professional associations, educational institutions or employers of professionals. Their responsibility has to be reassessed and must move toward a positive direction, particularly in the development and certification of continuing educational programs and providers. In many cases, this may raise questions of jurisdiction with colleges and other educational institutions that have been involved in the initial training of the practitioner.

Relationships with clients are changing as well. In many cases, the individual client or patient has given way to organizations or groups of individuals contracting for services, such as citizens of a community or a municipal or state agency. Even when the clients remain individuals, they are less in awe of the professional than once was the case and no longer passively accept mediocre treatment; witness the spread of malpractice suits against real estate agents, architects, accountants as well as corporate directors. Motivated by the consumer rights, supported by professional associations, and increasingly mandated by state legislation, continuing education for the professions now appears to be regarded as crucial for improvement of the services contributed by the professionals.

Shimberg (1980) indicates a whole new industry has arisen to deal with the problem created by mandatory continuing education, from developing and promoting courses to accrediting providers, recording participation and maintaining records. Some organizations appear to be concerned with the continuing education of the practitioner for the reasons that have little to do with the development of the individual. Most, however, attempt to provide programs specifically aimed to meet some professional or organizational needs, either within the framework of a specific job situation or on a broader scope.

Generally speaking, agencies conducting continuing education activities fall in three categories: employers of professionals, educational institutions and professional associations. Until recently it was fairly clear-cut as to how these agencies interacted with professionals. Employers usually sponsor in-house training programs, primarily to benefit the goals of the corporation, not the individual. Most emphasize skills development. Abrams (2003) cites programs such as project management and financial analysis for companies. Whatever the content level, the majority of programs are oriented to suit company practices and policies. He also cites recent evidence indicating that at least employers, in contrast with other providers, provide half of the continuing education in health care and that most management education is done by employers and by the training industry.

Furthermore, the central task of educators in employment settings is to improve participant's performance with respect to the mission of the agency. Houle (1980) describes the employers' ability to directly assess specific inadequacies of personal or collective service is perhaps the greatest strength of providing education within employment settings.

The weakness of this function of educational planning is likely to be far less proficient than for primary organizational goals. Employers can promote only on a limited vision on how to solve work related problems through learning activities. Since most programs are merged with human resource development activities, Nowlen (1988) notes that the educational strategy can become as incestuous and self-deceptive as the organizational culture that developed it.

Educational institutions, particularly those universities housing professional schools which educate people for entry into the profession, are likely to develop research based programs that are extensions of the regular curriculum. Abramson (1992), in his examination of factors affecting continuing education relating to engineering, contends that university developed programs lacked industrial applications, and that most programs respond to faculty needs before user needs. Nowlen (1988) on the other hand, maintains that the use of regular faculty to teach continuing education courses creates a synergy between the professional school curriculum and the courses designed for practicing professionals so that each is improved by what is learned from the other.

Higher educational institutions have a number of strengths as continuing professional providers. Universities are basically research oriented, and are a source of knowledge for most professions. Therefore it is appropriate that faculty members who develop and present this information should teach it to the practitioners through continuing education programs (Smutz, Crowe and Lindsay, 1986). These programs therefore lead to continuing education credits. At the same time universities have a large resident staff whose full time responsibility is giving instruction (Houle, 1980).

Currently, with the decline of intakes at the universities, the faculties are turning their energies to the education of practicing professionals. It must be mentioned that as a provider it has its weaknesses. The main weakness being that continuing professional education is not a core function of the universities, and funds are not allocated to these programs. It is more self-funded and being run by enthusiastic committee members where income is derived from participants. According to Knox (1987), this may contribute to the discontinuing of the programs if minimum numbers are not met. At the same time, some faculty members note that there are no incentives and rewards for faculty participation in the continuing education program, thus, declining to teach.

Sneed (1972) espoused that universities generally do not have the ability to link what is taught to practice. Even the continuing education representatives recognize that universities are separate from professional work settings and this cannot reinforce what is taught as well as other providers. Suleiman (1983) also emphasizes that universities are generally limited to their own faculty and facilities, and have limited ideas about pricing the programs and a general lack of marketing ideas.

The third type of agency offering continuing education for the professional is the professional association. Nowlen (1988) estimates there are at least three thousand national professional associations. These organizations are concerned with the development of their members in continuing education. Recently, most professional societies have restricted the continuing education activities to journal publications and annual meetings at which, scholarly research is disseminated through papers presented at various sessions (Houle, 1980).

Professional associations have a potent influence on the professional's career, beginning with the individual's selection for training. The important functions are accreditation, defining policies and practices, setting professional standards, approving related programs for members, policing their members on ethics and discipline, advocating professionalism and how licensing should take place.

As providers of continuing educators, professionals regard the association in common with employers association and educational universities as a source of continuing education activities to keep them updated. Houle (1980), in summarizing the contributions of the various agencies, provides a description of continuing profession education as,

> "…at a minimum, continuing professional education appears to be a complex of instructional systems, many of them heavily didactic, in which people who know something teach it to those who do not know it. The central aim of such teaching, which is offered by many providers, is to keep professionals up to date in their practice

The new role of the association in developing and accrediting continuing education for its constituents, are increasing at a fast rate, and the future concern will be for competency measures.

By the end of the 1980's professional providers have also seen widespread talk of a 'new paradigm' for industrial and commercial enterprises. At the core are notions of employee 'involvement' and 'commitment', 'flexibility' in roles and organizational structures, giving employees meaningful and responsible tasks, and utilizing and developing their skills, often in the context of product - focused 'teamwork' (Cruse, 1983). There is currently a challenge for action research in the design of work and work organization.

Paradoxically, the popularity of the 'new paradigm' is at the same time exposing some of the inadequacies of traditional socio-technical approaches. As the trend moves into the 1990's we find that research in the field of work organization demand developments in theory and practice. With the 'paradigm shift', professional providers have changed from their historic origin. They are now updating members on the 'awareness' on the 'happenings' around them. For professional members, they find that the updating process is like an 'awareness' of current knowledge, 'rediscovery' and also to reexamine change. The current trend of professional providers is now based on updating current issues. The organization too keeps high standards and also acts as certifiers of short programs. In some instances, holistic views of world issues and overseas expertise are invited to be shared, discussed and exchanged (Hohmann, 1980).

Some of the weakness of professional associations is the managing of the continuing education function. Houle (1980) argues that, different committees responsible for publication and education share the educational function. Since voluntary members giving their time after office hours run professional associations, the committee may only be responsible for a few programs, and thus the programs may not be important for the members.

Several other weaknesses include the staff members not being entrusted lead roles in carrying out the educational function. They are simply viewed as, 'seminar schedulers' according to Hohmann (1980) and with the changes to the board every year, strategic educational programming suffers. Suleiman (1983) notes that associations typically lack marketing ideas and pricing for their products. They too lack physical facilities such as meeting space, library and seminar rooms. Professional associations generally do not engage in inter-professional programming because they lack the political base to use association resources to address other professions Nowlen (1988).

Some of the professional providers, mentioned later in this book, have a dynamic governing council and a committed workforce and maintains high management standards, acts as a bridge between private and public sectors, a platform for free exchange of management knowledge and experience, and a partner for collaborative activities with other institutions.

In this context professional providers have updated their members professionally by keeping them informed of the current trends and issues. If a comparison is to be made regarding their activities since their inception, professional providers have come a long way in educating their members; but the question remains. Is this being done to enhance competency and professionalism among its members?

CPE and Collaboration

Houle (1980) suggests that various providers do what seems best and that the test of the marketplace will prevail. Current issues are complex and funding is difficult as CPE providers try to meet the needs of the professionals, community, business and the industry. Therefore, collaboration can be very advantageous. Information, ideas and resources can be pooled and duplication and harmful competition can be avoided. Beder (1984) suggests that collaboration can be a major agency expands strategy.

Partners can provide useful information on needs assessments and program evaluation, suggestions for curriculum development, participants, use of facilities and state of the art equipment, specialized staff and additional revenue from increased enrollments or from donations. If these resources are used by the education agency to provide quality continuing education programs, power and prestige can be increased and thus expanding options for programming and marketing.

Features of Positive Collaboration

In spite of the numerous benefits of collaboration, some relationships have failed to accomplish desired objectives and have been terminated, resulting in negative relationships among participants and providers, frustrations over unproductive investments of time and resources. Beder (1984) identifies four dominant themes that are important for successful relationships:

i.   Reciprocity: there must be a balance in giving and receiving resources as well as giving up domain and power. Each participant must perceive that resources less valued are being exchanged for resources that are more valued.

ii. System openness: external relationships should be actively sought, and there should be a receptiveness by external perspectives

iii. Trust and commitment: organizations cannot relinquish autonomy or perpetuate their collaborative relationship without trust and commitment. The level of trust and commitment can be affected by history of past collaborative efforts and the styles and personalities of the people involved.

iv. Structures: the compatibility of organizational structures and cultures is an important factor. Flat and flexible organizational structures help partners adapt to one another and create an environment of openness and receptivity.

Personal Factors

The people participating in collaborative relationships will contribute to its success or failure. The summary of a study that explored the benefits and problems of the collaboration of 247 organizations (Hohmann, 1985) identifies the individual behaviors of administrators as having significant consequences. The following behaviors characterize administrators who are effective collaborators:

i.   The ability to recognize the value and bargaining power of resources at hand and to identify outsiders who can contribute needed resources, the willingness to serve on committees and board outside their organizations and develop networks that could lead to collaboration opportunities, inclusive of planning and organizing skills.

ii. Individuals designated to represent an organization in collaboration, profoundly influence their organizations' perception of the relationship since information will be evaluated, interpreted and selectively communicated at the individual's discretion, and these representatives communicate frequently with their organizations and are very influential in decision-making processes.

Collaborative Strategies

Several authors (Bovard and Silling, 1986; Hemmings, 1984; Hohmann, 1985) suggest that the following strategies for developing productive collaborative relationships:

i. Survey the environment to locate possible partners, negotiate written agreements, allowing options and ideas, time frames and determine open channel of communication.

ii. Establish monitoring and evaluation procedures and channels to correct problems, and relying on any one of the collaborations can threaten the success of the program unless the partners are serious with the agreements. Although developing a program with partners is more time consuming than working alone (Cervero, 1984. p23), planning time will diminish as the organization becomes more experienced.

Providers of CPE, colleges and universities are practicing inter-organizational collaboration extensively in accordance to Cervero (1984). Some of the advantages include being prestige from being associated with a college or university, developing a close link between continuing educators and providers, high quality programs from shared resources, increased visibility for partners, sufficient number of participants, competent and professional staff.

Valentine (1984, p.65), supports that successful collaboration must demonstrate competent leadership, satisfy the diverse interests of program sponsors and program participants requires strong organizational, management, and interpersonal relations skills. Collaborative relationships are desirable because they expand the capacity of the participants to accomplish objectives by joining forces. In doing so they share resources, ideas, costs, leadership, and expertise and in the end everyone benefits (Hemmings, 1984).

Contextual Factors Associated with CPE Practice

CPE practices are almost done exclusively in the context of institutional settings. These settings may vary in size, complexity and purpose and determines the CPE practices of the professional provider. Each factor influences the organization in powerful ways what CPE providers do and how they do it. For example, in the case of the conference coordinator for a profit CPE organization will be judged by the number of registrants and net profit from her educational programs. Her institutional context offers clear and explicit guidelines for her vision of effective practice. Each specific organization has a unique set of values and resources and a particular history and culture. Continuing professional educators are attentive to these factors and guide their practice accordingly.

One of the major factors associated with professional associations is to conduct CPE programs and their ability to secure a wide array of talent, especially from their membership. Therefore, an associations' breadth of service and continuity of coverage and its educational program has a special capacity to deliver discrete and not sequential messages (Houle, 1980). Associations also have direct access to professionals who are seeking continuing education and are usually familiar with their learning needs. Associations too, engage in cost effective strategies by being a non-profit organization. Other factors influencing CPE practice is the continuing education function (Hohmanm, 1980). The educational function in a university setting typically shared by different divisions or committees responsible for publications, conventions, and standard type educational programs. The effect of this practice is that the educational program division may be responsible for only a few specific programs, and which may be considered not important by faculty because they can find these programs elsewhere. Continuing educators also suffer when they compete for internal resources with other divisions.

Suleiman (1983) notes that some of the contextual factors associated with the associations are insufficient marketing expertise and limited ideas on how to price their products. Associations may lack the physical facilities, such as a meeting space and a library that are necessary for educational ventures. Nowlen (1988) notes that associations do not engage in inter-professional programming because they lack the political base to use association resources to address other professions.

Factors influencing practice at employment setting, from the employers' viewpoint is relative convenience of scheduling and the minimization of lost work time due to attendance at programs outside the workplace. However, keeping participants' attention when attending an educational activity at the workplace can present several problems that stem from proximity to their work.

It is difficult for participants to focus on the educational program when they believe it is more important to work.

The institutional contexts strongly influence the focus of CPE practice. This occurs because the purposes of the parent agency are todetermine to a great extent the mission of the agency. Continuing educators themselves can help shape the mission and operating agenda for their agency. According to Knox (1981), there are a number of strategies available for them. Instead of carrying out the ends of the organization, they can work within the discretionary framework set up by the goals and resources of the organization.

The CPE process, with its complexity of contextual nature lends itself susceptible to many influencing factors. The quality of CPE programs depends on the suitability of the approach used, the methodology, the implementation, and the utilization of findings. Cervero (1988) suggested a set of common constraints and limitations of CPE that includes politics, ethics, time, and human resources.

CPE Practice

How do professionals develop their practice? What are the relationships between knowledge presented in CPE and use of that knowledge in the employment context? What impact does the context of professional practice have on the development of knowledge?

In this context, CPE and its application has been studied from a variety of perspectives, and many studies have tended to isolate or analyze the individual learner, rather than evaluating the learner within a particular context. Research in the transfer of knowledge (Broad and Newstrom, 1992) and diffusion of innovation (Rogers, 1995) has laid the groundwork for the study of learning and context.

Researchers and program planners (Black and Schell, 1995) have begun to understand that professionals engage in a more interactive process with the context of their practice and tend to combine elements of the context, information from continuing education and experience in practice to construct their own individual knowledge base. The use of knowledge in professional practice is an important issue in the field of adult education for a variety of reasons. First, employers and professionals in the United States spend billions of dollars annually on continuing education programs (Rowden, 1996).

Despite this huge investment of capital in continuing professional education programs the field of adult education can offer few assurances that the knowledge learned in these programs is linked to the context of practice. Secondly, professionals develop and change their practice with the intent of continually meeting clients' needs and expectations. For professionals to continue to meet the needs of their clients in society, a greater understanding of the connections between the context of practice and professional learning is needed.

As professionals continue to be integrated into organizations the linkages between context and practice need to be understood, defined and analyzed so that learning and professional practice can continue to grow in these new contexts. A major focus of continuing professional education programs is the mastery of specialized knowledge and the practice is influenced by the fact that the participants are adults who work in a particular setting. As such actual choices are made in everyday practice by continuing educators and professionals who are controlled by the environment they profess.

Schon (1987) argues that context of a professional practice is significantly different from other contexts. The commonalities of professional practice that set it apart from other human endeavors, their practices are structured in particular kinds of units of activity, cases, patient visits or lessons…a practice is made up of chunks of activity, divisible into more or less familiar types, each of which is seen as calling for the exercise of a certain kind of knowledge. Professionals are experts in their own way and helps in solving problems in their vocations. Schon (1983) describes professional activity that consists in instrumental problem solving made rigorous by the application of scientific theory and technique.

Thus professionals are seen as possessing a high degree of specialized expertise to solve well-defined problems. As such, systematic knowledge base can be developed more easily and applied with greater effectiveness and efficiency.

Practice is rigorous to the extent that it uses describable, testable, replicable techniques derived from scientific research, based on knowledge that is objective, consensual, cumulative and convergent (Schon, 1985).

On the other hand, contextual practice of CPE is not conducted in a laboratory where all conditions are controlled except for the educator's actions. If this is so, than the results will be quantified and measured and specific results will be shown, but practice is always conducted in a dynamic environment consisting of different personalities, shifting expectations, conflicting goals, and limited resources.

Sockett (1987) expounds that excellent practice cannot be characterized by a discrete set of knowledge of skills, but rather by an understanding of why educators do what they do and when they do it. At its root, practice not made up of measurable techniques but rather judgment, which is itself a form of knowledge. Schon (1983) contributed to the understanding of what professionals do through 'reflection'. The reflective practitioner is directed against 'technical-rationality' as to the grounding of professional knowledge. Technical-rationality is a positivist epistemology of practice. It is the dominant paradigm, which has failed to resolve the dilemma of rigor versus relevance confronting professionals. The notions of reflection-in-action and reflection-on-action were central to Schon's effort in this area. The former is sometimes described as 'thinking on our feet'. It involves looking to our experiences, connecting with our feelings, and attending to our theories in use.

It entails building new understandings to inform our actions in the situation that is unfolding. The practitioner allows himself to experience surprise, puzzlement, or confusion in a situation, which he finds uncertain or unique. He reflects on the phenomenon before him, and on the prior understandings, which have been implicit in his behavior. He carries out an experiment, which serves to generate both a new understanding of the phenomenon and a change in the situation (Schon, 1983)

We can link this process of thinking on our feet with reflection-on action. This is done later, after the encounter. Workers may write up recordings, talk things through with a supervisor and so on. The act of reflecting-on-action enables us to spend time exploring why we acted as we did, what was happening in a group and so on. In doing so, we develop sets of questions and ideas about our activities and practice. Practitioners build up a collection of images, ideas, examples and actions that they can draw upon. Schon, like Dewey (1933, p.123) saw this as central to reflective thought:

> "When a practitioner makes sense of a situation he perceives to be unique, he sees it as something already present in his repertoire. To see this site as that one is not to subsume the first under a familiar category or rule. It is, rather to see the unfamiliar, unique situation as both similar and different with respect to what. The familiar situation functions as a precedent, or a metaphor, or…an exemplar for the unfamiliar one (Schon 1983, p.138)

Schon's (1983) contention is inadequate that practitioners merely possess declarative knowledge. Professionals need to excel in their field as experts. The appropriate knowledge needed for effective practice is to know how to connect continuous learning, plans techniques, ideas and knowledge to make judgment in the uncertain and often changing contexts of practice or indeterminate areas of higher learning. Daley (2001) describes this as linking knowledge to practice. CPE practice does not exist in isolation from the real world of practice. There are no standardized solutions, which can be applied by practitioners. The critical viewpoint rejects rigid prescriptions for the exemplary practice of professional (Cervero, 1988). A contextual understanding of the matter is urged. The critical viewpoint emphasizes the need to continually come out with new ideas that make professional practice effective.

Professionals who are unaware of their own shortcomings fail to excel. They are unable to create open communication or inquire themselves. As inquirers frame the problem of the situation, they determine the features to which they will attend, the order they will attempt to impose on the situation, the directions in which they will try to change it. In this process, they identify both the ends to be sought and the means to be employed (Schon, 1983). They try to understand why they are predisposed to learning in a particular way, which is their personal cognitive style. Argyris and Schon's (1996) process of knowing in model-11 provide a realistic abstraction of the actual experiences of professionals in the following steps:

i. They gather valid information from practice.

ii. They exercise free and informed choice on practices.

iii. They exhibit an internal commitment to their chosen course of actions while constantly monitoring its implementation

iv. They make preferred choices and commitment.

v. They evaluate their decisions.

That is deliberate action must follow as without action there is no learning (Pedler, 1997). Action learning (Revans, 1982) is a development approach that treats the task itself as learning, as an opportunity for individuals to reflect and make progress on their problems while working at their tasks. In the meantime, when professionals make sense of a situation, they reconcile, integrate, or choose among conflicting appreciation of a situation so as to construct a coherent problem worth solving (Schon, 1987).

Although the responsibility for improving practice must rest ultimately with the individual continuing educators, the achievement of this goal can be facilitated by individuals who see themselves as part of the collective enterprise of CPE.

CHAPTER 5

CPE AND PLANNED CHANGE

Change and CPE

CPE is a relatively new field of study. The term itself has only come into common use since the 1960s. A major contribution to establishing CPE as a distinct area of study was Houle's (1980) scholarly overview of the policies and practices of seventeen professions in the United States. The central theme of this book was that the professions were in a state of crisis, and that a new paradigm of CPE was necessary to resolve it.

He further argued that the ad hoc mixture of association conventions and meetings, journals, sales representations, and occasional formal educational activities that constituted the state of CPE should be replaced by a more systematic approach and a much greater commitment to lifelong learning among the professions (Houle, 1980).

Although Houle was not clear on the course of action to achieve this new paradigm, he did provide a comprehensive description of the issues and thoughtful discourse on possible alternatives. The crisis that concerned Houle arose during the 1960s and 1970s as the mystique of the professions began to fade in the public's eye. The reasons given for this decline included real and imagined shortcomings in professional competence, concern over the ability of professions to regulate themselves, and the perception of some that professional elites were oppressing the powerless by controlling service markets.

Also during this time, professionals themselves were becoming increasingly concerned over the competence of lesser able colleagues. Houle saw that continuing education would play an increasingly important role in addressing these issues. He cautioned, however, that merely increasing traditional continuing education activities, which typically involved simple lectures or classroom formats, were not likely to be effective or efficient in bringing about the needed level of reform.

Houle encouraged research into forms of learning, including self-directed learning that would result in actual improvements in practice. Houle feared that political expediency combined with false assumptions about learning could result in ill-conceived mandatory continuing education requirements for professionals. Unfortunately many of Houle's concerns were realized as increasing numbers of professional regulatory agencies implemented policies based on traditional educational practices. Driven by more recent research, a reexamination of past assumptions is underway in continuing medical education (Fox, 1984).

Among Houle's contributions to CPE is his own research into modes of learning among professionals. He identified three, the first of which he referred to as *inquiry*. This was defined as the process of creating a new synthesis, ideas, techniques, policies, or strategies of action. Sometimes these involved structured activities, such as seminars or discussion groups, but more often learning was a by-product of efforts directed toward creating a policy, working out compromises, or projecting plans. *Instruction* was Houle's second mode of learning, which he described as involving instructor led activities commonly associated with education. The third model was referred to as *performance*, which was the process of internalization of skills and knowledge that took place with repetition in practice.

Houle's modes of learning are typical of the descriptive nature of his work. They contribute to our general understanding of the professions but do not address the how and why of professional learning nor the subtle relationships between learning and change in practice. Nonetheless, his work has been critical in establishing CPE as a distinct form of adult education and has provided subsequent scholars a framework for inquiry and a standard for scholarship.

Building on the foundations of Houle's work, Cervero (1988) offered another approach to understanding the nature of CPE. According to Cervero (1988) society and educators have viewed the professions from either a functional or conflict perspective. Functionalists see professionals as possessing a high degree of specialized expertise to solve well-defined problems.

In this context continuing education is instrumental in helping professionals to improve their knowledge, competence, and performance, which is assumed to result in a higher quality service to clients. CPE thus becomes a primarily technical process performed in support of enhancing the power and responsibility of the vocation (Houle, 1980).

According to Cervero, most continuing professional educators act within this frame of reference, and their efforts are generally directed toward incremental changes in practices. Proponents of the conflict viewpoint, such as Illich (1977) and Larson (1977), contend that professions create a need for their services and strive to control the public's access to competing services. This view suggests that educational interventions must take place at a social-structural level, not at the individual level, in order to weaken the professionals' power over the public. The role of CPE in this paradigm is to advocate systemic change (Cervero, 1988)

Cervero (1988) offered an alternative to the purely functionalist or radical conflict viewpoints. He suggested a critical approach in which one concedes the need for the special knowledge and competence of professions while recognizing the lack of consensus about professional quality and standards. Cervero suggested that CPE should both address the competency needs of the profession and encourage professionals to reflect upon the use of that knowledge. Critical educators should ask, why should professionals have this knowledge and to what end will it be put to practice (Cervero, 1988).

Consistent with Cervero's critical view, Schon (1987) observed that professionals often must make decisions concerning ambiguous situations that fall outside of the profession's knowledge base and the individual professional's zone of mastery. In such cases, human values and interests and personal experiences of professionals have a significant influence on practice decisions.

Schon further suggested that professionals engage in a process of simultaneous reflection and action toward resolving these ambiguous situations. Educators should, therefore, work toward enhancing the professionals' reflective abilities. Several other scholars have contributed to the general knowledge base of CPE. Significant among them are the works of Knox and Nowlen. Knox has written on a variety of issues including reasons why professionals participate in continuing education (Knox, 1981). He offered a theory of motivation based upon professionals' concern for proficiency in practice (Knox, 1986).

According to Knox (1986) when professionals perceive a gap in their proficiency, they become motivated to learn in order to reduce their anxiety. This theory further suggested that if gaps in proficiency are perceived as very small or very large the professional will be less likely to engage in learning. Nowlen too has contributed to the general knowledge of CPE. He brought attention to the importance of considering personal characteristics and professional culture in the planning of CPE. He argued eloquently that these two factors intertwine like a double helix and in doing so affect both learning and performance (Nowlen, 1988).

The works of Houle, Cervero, Knox, Nowlen and others (Argyris & Schon, 1974; Baskett & Marsick, 1992; Bennett & Legrand, 1990; Davis & Fox, 1994; Fox, Mazmanian, & Putnam, 1989; Grotelueschen, 1985; Scanlan, 1985; Smutz & Queeny, 1990) constitute the foundation of the emerging field of CPE. Each scholar presented a somewhat different vision of CPE, thus the picture is yet complete. But what is clearly evident in their work is a shared belief that the overarching purpose of continuing professional education is change.

Intentional Change and Learning

The literature presented thus far supports the proposition that individuals make intentional changes as a consequence of either external or internal forces or their interaction. The works of adult learning researcher and theorist, Tough (1982) added additional support and revealed the enormous degree to which people engage in intentional change. They further revealed the instrumental role learning plays toward achieving these changes. Learning in this case refers to behavior directed toward obtaining information and skills rather than internal psychological processes.

Although Tough's research was conducted with the general population, it contributed directly to the study of change and learning in the professions in several important ways. It provided a model for the study of change and learning from the perspective of the learners. It showed that in addition to intentionally deciding to make changes, people most often plan and direct their own learning activities. It clearly demonstrated that learning involves both formal and informal learning resources, with the latter being far more commonly used; and in a majority of cases studied, the motivating force for learning was the desire to improve performance or solve immediate problems related to work.

Finally, it suggested that professionals might be intensely involved in changing and learning, as the level of activity was found to increase with education and social classifications.

Studies of Change and Learning

The first and most significant study of change and learning among professionals was the Physicians' Change Study conducted by Fox, Mazmanian, and Putnam (1989). In 1987 a group of continuing medical educators conducted interviews with approximately 375 physicians in the United States and Canada. The doctors were asked to identify recent changes in their practice or life and to recall associated learning activities, if any had occurred. They found that most changes involve some degree of new learning, which varies according to the types of changes and the motivations driving them. Many continuing education programs are designed to help individuals to change. Change is likely to continue to dominate our future lives, institutions and society. It is the responsibility of continuing educators and educational agencies, as change-agents, to help people understand change as it affects their lives.

Change means to alter or modify something and can evolve naturally or by deliberate planning. A natural change is automatic and follows the path of history and evolution. That change is not managed, does not have (proper) direction and goal, and does not use valid knowledge and available resources.

Change that evolves naturally can have either a positive or negative impact on development. The idea of planned change refers to the deliberate efforts made to alter behavior of an individual, a group or a system. Nadler (1998) view planned change as a deliberate and collaborative process involving a change-agent and a client system. It is a method that employs social technology and available resources to help solve problems of man and societies. Houle (1972) describes planned change as a purposeful decision and deliberate effort to improve a system. In making the improvement, he suggests that the help of an outside agent be solicited.

Some key elements related to plan change are: conscious effort to alter performance, desirable goal, collaborative effort between the change-agent (the party who provides professional guidance) and the client system (the party whose behavior is to be changed) as well as employment of all available resources. Planned change may be conceptualized as a conscious and purposive effort (collaborative between the client system and the change-agent) to alter performance or behavior of a client system towards desirable goals by using available resources. There are a few key ideas involved in promoting planned change. They are client system, change-agent, change relationship and leverage point. The client system is the party that is being helped or whose behavior is to be altered. The client system may be an individual, a group, an organization, a community or a society that is aiding or leading this change process.

CPE and the Change Agent

The change-agent is referred to as the party that provides professional guidance. The change agent can be a system, a group or an individual. The agent's role as the professional in the process of planned change includes the appraisal of the client system's problems, client motivation and choosing the specific techniques and mode of behavior that are appropriate to each phase in the change relationship.

The change-agent is also expected to establish and maintain the helping relationship and guiding the phases of change. The change relationship refers to the relationship between the client system and the change-agent. This is a situation where both parties arrive at a decision to work together toward the process of achieving the desired goal of the planned program.

The leverage point is the starting point in the helping process towards the proposed change. The change-agent can use the selected persons or subgroups, which are influential and more favorable to the change program as the leverage point. The agent's leverage point can also be strategically located, functional or a structural component of the client system.

CPE and Promoting Change

Key elements that are critical for the success of change in a program may be promoted through planned change and involves the following strategies: developing the needs for change, zeroing on change problems, establishing goals and intention of action, committing to action and stabilizing the change.

Development of a Need for Change

In order for change to occur, the potential client usually experiences problems that create tension within the system. To trigger the change, the client system must be brought into a state of problem awareness. Once the client is aware of the problem, they can be motivated to desire a change and recognize the need to seek outside help. The change process at this phase may occur through three different situations. It can occur when the change agent brings the need for change to the client system, or the client system discovers there is a need to get help, or a third party identifies the needs of the client system and then links the client system to the change agent.

Zeroing in on the Problem

This phase of change usually deals with the collection, analysis and interpretation of data about the client system's problems. The change-agent will work with the client system to clarify problems and make diagnosis. The process of change will depend upon the understanding and acceptance of the diagnosis by the client.

Establishing Goals and Intention of Action

The change process usually involves translation of the diagnostic insights into ideas of alternative means of action followed by the direction of change being defined. This phase denotes the program designing stage, which includes committing resources and identifying action steps to be taken.

Committing To Action

This refers to the implementation process in affecting change. Plans are launched into practical and actual situation. A commitment to action is a direct commitment to change.

Stabilization of Change

This is the phase where change has been accomplished, stabilized and remains a permanent character of the client system. The mechanisms involved in the process include the confirmation of practice or behavior change by other members of the client system, feedback and reinforcement. The planned change may be stabilized when it is supported by the structural changes of the system. At this stage, the role of change-agents is critical to ensure planned change takes place smoothly. Boone (1985) lists five process-based tasks to ensure the success of the key elements critical to the process of the change program. They are:

i. The change-agent must utilize various strategies and techniques in marketing both the planned program and the planned action.

ii. The change-agent must identify, mobilize, develop and utilize resources both human and material, to implement and carry through the adult learning experiences enumerated in the plans of action effectively.

iii. The change-agent must make provisions for on-going monitoring of planned learner experiences.

iv. The change-agent must provide for continuous reinforcement of the learners and the facilitators.

v. The change-agent must maintain sensitivity to the need for and the willingness to adapt or redirect learner experiences like monitoring, feedback and their own observations, which expose the need for change.

vi. The change-agent, both formal and informal, is the source of power and authority and act as legitimers. Therefore, when social change is introduced into a social system, the change-agent needs to be involved in legitimization.

Institutions are important aspects of structural-functionalism. Important social institutions such as religion, youth club, professional association and providers, etc. can help to promote social change. Since each of these institutions is established based on similar interest, conflict perspective can promote change that appeal to the interest group. Another aspect that can be identified in a society is the communication process and structure. There is a need to identify key communicators to help the change-agent promote change. Authority and opinion leaders can help extend new ideas to the rest of society. Key communications can be established at various locations in the society to provide a system of interpersonal communication network.

From a conflict perspective, the concept of dialectical process can be useful in the promotion of change. In identifying the needs for change, the change-agent and clientele should be engaged in a dialogue so that those involved are able to problematize, i.e. to describe the problematic situation, define problems, analyze them and design solutions.

According to Freire (1972), dialogue and problematization are parts of the process of conscientization; that is, when the client becomes critically aware. In other words, dialogue, problematization, and conscientization are processes are involved in raising consciousness to those who want to change their status quo. Planned change is a change, which is derived from purposeful decisions to affect improvement in the client system. Such change can be achieved with the help of professional guidance from the change-agent.

CPE and Training

In order to achieve the constant support, which the change-agents need, there is a need for more training for supervisors and project officers training appropriate to their proper role of resource persons working alongside their development workers and instructors. Those concerned with programs of 'staff development' have identified two main models: a 'developmental' (bottom-up and problem-solving) model and a 'deficit' (top-down, input-based) model. While low skill functions will be replaced by new technology, the remaining workforce would inevitably update knowledge or undergo technology transfer in an intensive course to match skills required in their new environment (Nowlen, 1988). The former is more concerned with the needs of the person, the latter with the needs of the organization he or she serves. Much the same is true of the training of supervisors. They may be molded to fit the needs of the program and the agency, or they may be made innovative and free to exercise judgment in the fulfillment of their role of helper of change-agents.

Such training, if it is really to help the change agents, needs to be pragmatic and practical rather than textbook and academic. Supervisors exist to serve rather than control and instruct the change-agents. In this capacity, they need to have had some experience of development to be good practitioners rather than good theoreticians. Theory and development, as in adult education, grows out of practice more than practice out of theory. Supervisors and project officers thus need to be trained practically in development. And this in turn creates demand for new patterns of training the trainers for development: training is best conducted by those who are themselves experienced in the problems of being supervisor and of being a change-agent rather than by experts in the theory of development.

Unfortunately, this bottom-up approach to training is in many cases a long way off. What usually exists is a top-down model, in which academics tell the supervisors what they should know and these in turn pass it down to the change-agents. The trainers set the format, the timing and the content of the training rather than helping the change-agents to plan their own training.

CPE and Innovation

Many training programs are designed to limit initiative, to discourage decision-making by the trainees, and to encourage conformity to an ideal. They set out to create a model extension worker or change-agent, to foster the adoption of approved methods of animation (demonstration, role play or simulation, etc.); they try to 'give all the answers'. Rarely do training programs set out to encourage the change-agents to innovate, to solve problems, to identify for themselves resources, which can help them.

But the demand for innovative change-agents on a mass scale is bringing about changes in the content and methods of these initial and in-service training programs. These latter training programs may be analyzed in terms of our developmental model.

They start with the existing state, the intentions and aspirations of the change-agents, with what they want to learn rather than with topics chosen by the supervisors, trainers and agencies.

The articulation of these concerns by the change-agents will serve to heighten their awareness as they reflect critically on their role as change-agent, the resources available to them, and their own needs and aspirations. Such programs seek to develop the knowledge, skills and understandings necessary for an effective change-agent – not just a limited range of communication skills and extension techniques, but a deeper understanding of the process of changing society, including identifying barriers and resources in their environment. They pay attention to attitude formation as well as knowledge change-attitudes that the change-agents hold towards themselves, towards the task, and towards the participant groups.

They practice decision-making by the trainees, building confidence in the change-agents to plan their own learning and they build in programs of active learning (instead of merely listening and watching) during the training programs-activities, which will help the trainees to become more effective change-agents.

To be effective, change-agents need to become the participants in the development process themselves; and the supervisors, academics and 'experts' who train them also need to experience development as they in their turn learn how to train. For education and training is a form of development - and those who experience it will make well-developed workers.

CHAPTER 6

CPE, PROFESSIONALS AND PROFESSION

The Professionals

CPE includes ways in which professionals enhance their proficiencies related to these characteristics as well as to their individual collective efforts to specify standards of practice related to these characteristics. It includes both mastery of procedures important to professional practice and consideration of the goals and standards. A clear definition of professional is elusive. Becker (1962) examined the efforts of social scientists since 1900 to define the term "professional" and concluded that no one definition or set of occupations can be acceptable to all. A list of characteristics developed by Flexner (1915) is, however, representative of most of these efforts:

i. Involves intellectual judgment by individual practitioners.
ii. Learned activity with a constantly growing base of knowledge and responsibility for learning and research that continues beyond initial preparation.
iii. Practical activity.
iv. Involves special techniques.
v. Organized for the purpose of controlling the quality of the profession.

The literature also shows that during the 1930s when Flexner offered these criteria, distinctions between the professions and vocations were no doubt easier to recognize. Only a few vocations, such as medicine, law, clergy, teaching and to some extent, architecture and engineering, were commonly thought as professions. Today many vocations can claim they are professions within Flexner's definition. At the same time, Houle offered an approach to categorizing professions involving thirteen dynamic processes rather than static characteristics. His scheme recognized that professions, even the established ones, are always in a state of professionalizing (Houle, 1980). In the meantime Cervero (1988), in quantifying professionals, state that professionals learn through books, discussions with colleagues, formal and informal educational programs and from the rigor of everyday practice. This simplistic and broad description of professionals has been differentiated through several approaches.

Flexner (1915) describes concepts of professionalization as being based on static approach and differentiates occupation from a profession in which a profession; is an intellectual operation with large individual responsibility, and possessing certain professional characteristics:

    i.   Sets to achieve a define purpose with outcomes and is goal oriented

    ii. Possesses techniques that are communicable through education and scope is given for the application of intelligence tends to be self-organized. There is a definite organization, i.e. it develops a distinct class-consciousness.

In contrast to Flexner's (1915) concept of professionalization, Butcher and Strauss (1961), Larson (1979) and Houle (1980) stress that professionalization is based on the process or emergent approach, which sees jobs evolving into professions through a process. This concept approach provides a profession various segmentation or specialization which in turn gives rise for conflicts to take place due to differences in value systems. The value system is detailed below:

    i.   Sense of mission that is unique especially to the segment within the profession.

    ii. Diversity in work activities within the profession.

    iii. Methodological differences due to the different techniques by the specialties divergence of interest gives rise to the formation of many associations. Those who control the professional association also control the aspects of public relations.

The above process, according to Houle (1980), contributes to continuous refinement of ethical standards and characteristics of team concept through lifelong learning. Profession, in its ideal term, is defined as a high status occupation of highly trained experts performing a specialized role in society. According to Houle (1980), professional competency could be developed and improved through the process of CPE. The emerging concept of Houle (1980), Butcher and Strauss (1961) strikes the author as the best analysis because the concept evolves value system through conflict and diversity.

Thus professing mixed characteristics leads to working together for a common goal through life long learning and continuous improvement into the twentieth century. Following the explanation of the above process, selected professional providers members or clients in this study, can be categorized as professionals. As professional members of these selected professional providers, the members are expected to engage in continuous learning activities and acquire expertise to provide professional services to the profession and to the community at large.

The Profession

Literature search traces the origin of the true profession in America to the ministry. The word profession as we now use it evolved from the action of ministers professing their commitment to selfless service to the church. Nowlen (1988) argues that the professions of law, medicine and engineering acquired some of the attributes and status of the ministry as they emerged in the later half of the nineteenth century. It is this calling to selfless service that separates professions from vocations.

Flexner and Friedson have been trying to define, "profession" for a long time. Flexner's (1915,) static approach distinguishes professions from other occupations. He identified the following six characteristics as essential for an occupation to claim professional status. Professions must involve intellectual operations, derive their materials from science, involve definite and practical ends, possess an educationally communicable technique, tend to self-organization and must be altruistic.

On the other hand, Friedson (1986) argues that a process approach to distinguish the professions from other occupations stands very clear. The process approach is based on the premise that the professions are necessary to the smooth and orderly functioning of society. To this effect, society rewards professionals with high status and money for their highly valued work (Barber, 1963; Parsons, 1949). Friedson (1986) proposes that for an occupation to be classified as a profession, some amount of higher education must be a prerequisite to employment.

The rationale is that formal knowledge creates qualification for particular jobs, from which others lack such qualification are routinely excluded. Such a circumstance is likely to mean that those occupations have developed a coherent organization that succeeds in carving out a labor-market shelter. Finally, true professions are self-referenced sub cultures. Members of each profession hold a unique set of common values and speak a special language not easily understood by outsiders.

Nowlen (1988) defines professional culture as the context within which individual meaning making and personal growth takes place. Nowlen described the factors affecting professional performance as a double helix of a professional's personal history intertwined with the professional culture. This concept is supported by emerging theories of organizational learning that suggest that members of an organization and the organization itself can learn and that this learning is affected by organizational structure and climate (Senge, 1990). Nowlen's concept has special significance for CPE and this book. It suggests that understanding change, professions, professionals and professional providers and the study of CPE must recognize the unique contextual factors associated in this study.

CHAPTER 7

CPE IN MALAYSIA

Although contextual factors associated with CPE practices have been the subject of much research, most of the focus has been on comparing the method practiced with theory and models prescribed in the literature. This book was designed to understand how contextual factors shape continuing professional practices of selected professional providers in Malaysia thus resulting in some information for the need for CPE practices among practicing professional providers, especially in Malaysia and generally in the global context. For a developing country like Malaysia, there is a major impact on its importance of adult and continuing education programs especially so when it is becoming a center of excellence for education and training globally.

In this context the expansion of management, human resource and training activities has created greater demands and expectations in the industry, thus placing pressure on continuing education providers and change agents. Professional providers are being challenged to improve their professional proficiency and competency with special focus on CPE.

CPE has not been the subject of much research in recent years, especially in Malaysia. Little or no concern has been given to the development of CPE in Malaysia. CPE is also at its infancy stage in Malaysia and the potential for growth is enormous.

There are many different professional providers providing adult and continuing programs in Malaysia. They can be classified from the core programs they provide for the clients.

The following chapter is divided into three sections: first, the profile and CPE practices of nine selected professional providers; the second description helps us to understand what are the contextual factors associated with CPE practices of the selected professional providers and the third description answers how these contextual factors influence the development of CPE practices in these selected professional providers in Malaysia.

Profile and CPE Practices of Providers

Each description consists of a brief background of the provider's mission, program, and how their CPE practices were approached. To respect confidentiality, the providers have been named from providers A through to I. Table 1 depicts the respondents interviewed from each provider, the type of provider and type of documents collected from the providers.

Table 1: Profile of Providers & Source of Document

	Profile of Providers		Source of Document	
Provider	Respondent Interviewed	Number of Years Attached	Type of Provider	
A	V P – Education & Training	10	Human Resource Institute	Annual report, magazines, brochures
B	V P– Training & Education	5	Institute for Training & Development	Profile of institute, magazines, program brochures.
C	Director – Technical Research	6	Institute of Chartered Secretaries & Administrators	Profile, bulletins, program brochures, website.
D	President	7	Real Estate	Profile, magazines, brochures, annual report.

	Profile of Providers		Source of Document	
Provider	Respondent Interviewed	Number of Years Attached	Type of Provider	
E	Manager – Acting – Division	7	Management Accounting	Profile, magazines, brochures, annual report.
F	Manager – Education	8	Financial Accounting	Profile, magazines, brochures.
G	Asst. Director – Extension School	5	Public University – Extension School	Profile website, brochures, magazines.
H	Professor – ManagementSchool	7	Public University – Extension School	Profile, website, program brochures, magazines.
I	Dean – Professor of Management	7	Private University	Website, profile, program brochures, magazines.

Provider A - Profile

Provider A was established in 1975 as a sole national institute in Malaysia as part of an interest group for human resource and training. Provider A is the leading institute for quality training and education in human resource management in Malaysia. Provider A has trained approximately 5,000 competent HR professionals and practitioners in both private and public sectors since its establishment. To date, Provider A has over 2000 individual members and 171 corporate members. Provider A has an elected council consisting of 10 members and is volunteers. The president and the council members make the decisions on how the institute would be run from time to time. Provider A is affiliated with the World Federation of Personnel Management Associations, the International Federation of Training and Development Organizations, the Asian Regional Training & Development Organization and several other similar bodies. It has branches in other states in Malaysia.

The standard of quality for Provider A is proven through the achievement of the ISO 9002 certification by SIRIM in July 1998. Among Provider A's objectives are:

- To serve as the national organization for persons concerned with or involved for interest in human resource management / development
- To foster and promote efficient and effective personnel management practices, particularly to suit the Malaysian needs.
- To encourage the study and research into the art and science of human resource management and to provide the necessary facilities for its development.
- To promote and safeguard the interests of the institute and its members and the dignity of the profession.
- To ensure that members adhere to the institute's code of ethics.

Some of the training programs or initiatives undertaken by Provider A as seen in the documents, brochures and catalogues are monthly tea-talks, certificate and diploma programs in human resource management and industrial relations, annual conferences, human resource consultancy and publication.

The institution is a non-profit organization catering specifically for the human resource profession.

Provider A - CPE Practices

The business scenario seems to be on the decline due to two reasons, namely, competition with small time consulting firms and non-marketing of current products due to shortage of marketing staffs. Adding to this during the economic slowdown, many programs were either postponed or cancelled. As such, "*CPE is important to the individual and the institution and they should subscribe to it at four levels, namely, job description must be aligned to company goals, different areas of training must be identified, training must be conducted on a timely basis and the learning by the individual must be in line to company's goals.*" The organizing of 'updates' of CPE is non-existence because of objections from the members, mostly human resource and training professionals. Accordingly, the members are old and are resistant to change.

In short, they do not want to try any new methods. There is also no particular role played by the institution to manage advice and guide members on CPE. They are trying to model the works of the Chartered Institute of Personal and Development, UK, but it would take time. Currently, most programs are 'run of the mill' programs, like tea-talks and get-togethers, but even with that, the response for such programs are very slow from members.

The Professional Development Committee has been around for two years. It lacks a good committee with experience to run and manage CPE programs. Since this is a voluntary position, they tend not to push them. According to the respondent, the institution has resources for CPE, library, training rooms and an academic senior manager to run the center, but comes without experience. The programs run on a self-financing basis, and the various committees are required to submit their proposals to the treasurer who allocates budgets for carrying out programs.

Most of the time the institution runs on the fees received from the 2000 members and from profits made (if any) from the programs. When asked about evaluation, *"There is no system of monitoring and evaluation of CPE, only reaction sheets at the end of the program and a certificate of attendance upon completion of the course."* On a long-term program, the participants would obtain certificates and diplomas. Currently, there seems to be an attempt of collaboration with other bodies, especially independent training providers.

There is no policy on CPE other than the objectives on education and training in the constitution as documented in their reports, and most programs are run on a generic basis. As there is no program developer, an executive is required for current running of professional programs and managing all training functions. The ownership of CPE is thought to be on the institution and the provider, and they should work in tandem to streamline the programs for the individuals, who follow the standards set by the professional development committee. On comparing the institution with other professional bodies, there are positive signs at emulating them. Some of the professional bodies they are looking at are the Chartered Institute of Personal and Development, UK and the Society for Human Resource Management, USA since these institutions have structured programmes on CPE.

Accordingly, some of the challenges faced by the institution are a common policy on CPE, structured CPE programs, certification of trainers and getting them 'updated' with the latest knowledge and skills of the profession. At the same time, the institution should run and manage CPE efficiently with allocated financial resources.

In summary the CPE practices of Provider A can be characterized by serving, fostering and promoting human resource practices, encouraging and advising members of the importance of attending professional updates, allocating budgets, facilities and resources for members' convenience. On the other hand there is no practice of compulsory attendance of CPE programs, or program planning and evaluation. The practice of collaboration is still at an early stage.

Provider B - Profile

Provider B was formed in 1994 as a non-profit, non-government professional organization. They have not only grown from strength to strength but are also reckoned as a leader in training & development. This is a break away from provider A, who has 400 professional members and 70 corporate members.

Provider B has attained its current status and recognition as a society of equal standing with that of any other professional bodies due mainly to its active participation and contributions toward national training and development strategies and policies. Provider B's business linkages in the field of training and development with regional and worldwide organizations have augured well for its reputation in the international training community.

Besides being involved in high profiled image creating activities, Provider B's achievements in serving its members and others in the training public locally have been commendable. Among the varied activities and projects that Provider B has earned its name all this while is through its training and education programmes, which have been widely accepted as one of its kind in the local market.

Some of the activities Provider B has embarked on for the benefit of its members are tea-talks, workshops, seminars, foundation certificates in training and development, and annual trainers' evenings, a social and networking event. To upkeep its enviable status as the national organization for training and development, Provider B had also organized its first Annual Training Conference and Exposition in 1996, and intends to make this a yearly event. Above all, the project that is undertaken currently is the certificate and diploma in Applied Training and Development, which is in collaboration with a local institution of higher learning and would be launched in the very near future.

Some core beliefs of the provider include:
- To be the first in implementing any training and development initiatives
- To develop potential human resource to meet its mission and goals
- To add values to the individual and organizational potential that leads to improved performance
- To develop professionalism in the human resource development field for their stakeholders

Provider B has an elected council consisting of about 15 members, led by the President. All council members are volunteers. The institution has about 400 members and during the recession this number dropped drastically. The objective of the institution is to enhance trainer professionalism by conducting short courses, long term certificate and diploma programs and to organize conventions for the members.

Provider B - CPE Practices

During the recent slowdown, the institution made some changes with their programs, instead of 'stand up and deliver' they changed their mode to 'on-line' programs, providing new ideas and 'updating' on the new 'flavor of the season'. With the recent business changes, the individual/trainer needs to update themselves with new products and approaches. They need to be more marketable and need to change with the time. New knowledge, skills and attitude need to be looked at, as organizations are displacing individuals and are only keeping those who are able to multi-skill.

CPE is important to the organization and the individual, because businesses are dynamic, and change takes place. They need to look into professional updates with new learning packages and should encourage self-learning contracts. It was also lamented that, *"There are no opportunities in the continuum of age 55, as new activities and new changes takes place, i.e. retirement."* Learning is life-long. It's not a new concept. It's been there all the time. Lifelong means one also has to cater for people who have stopped working and who are retired. This is further argued as a little disturbing in the sense that there is not much that is available or even government provided for this age group. People after 55 who live another 15-20 years too have to learn to adapt themselves to new activities, to the changing environment and there could be a lot of these development opportunities offered to them. Libraries are now so restricted that everyone has to up to RM250.00 just to go to the library. " A senior citizen should be allowed to go to the library, to keep himself updated at all times.

The institution does not organize CPE per-se, but organizes updates through tea-talks, where members have the opportunities to share ideas with their fellow peers; but even so, tea meetings responses are very slow. Trainers are busy; they feel that learning is low priority. This boils down to their need, and the client's don't insist on certain standards of the trainers. They don't conduct any return on investments on training and therefore anything goes.

The company, some time ago, brought about compulsory CPE for their members, but was put aside when some of the members complained that this was an obstacle being placed in their way. The institution developed some competencies together with a code of ethics for trainers and this was then collaborated with INTAN, the government-training house, but nothing has officially come out of it yet.

The role played by the institution to manage CPE is very minimal. Since their CPE's are just tea-talks, dinner meets and exchange of ideas, it is done informally and there are no formal requirements. The staff encourages members to update, without force. It is the desire of the institution to have a structured process so that all the members will go through proper CPE to update themselves.

The institution runs on a low budget with two volunteer staff. It rents a half floor from one of her members' personal properties. There are no library facilities or training and meeting rooms, but there is an intention to have an Internet corner for the members, as it only requires a small space. Currently, the institution runs programs that are self-financing and depends on her member's annual fees to run operations.

The institute has no policy on CPE; therefore it's not compulsory for members to update themselves. It is of the that the ownership of CPE should be with all the stakeholders, especially the organization, provider and the individual The organization should have onus of CPE so as to create a learning organization, but the individual must own it because it's his life goals that is at stake and the provider to provide the need for the institution.

Most programs run by the institution are based on competency development but is generic. Some of the programs include Train the Trainer, certificate and diploma programs in Training and Development and other soft skills programs. At the end of this program, participants get a certificate of attendance. Collaborative attempts with the local universities, like University of Malaya and Sunway University College to run their certificate and diploma programs are currently in progress.

When comparing with other professional bodies, the institution is not prone to conducting CPE programs because there is no legal entity to it. It is emphasized that, the medical and the engineers group are liable to any mistake and could be sued for negligence, but the profession is still a young profession, which does not need to be mandatory CPE. Moreover, there needs to be a legislation to legalize trainers in the country and standards to be drawn up; and even then there is a need to have enforcement. The Ministry of Human Resources have their hands full in managing the training funds and even with the legislation they have problems coping with the contributors of the fund.

The Human Resource Development Board should look into the updating and upgrading of the trainers. The board should look into the evaluation sheets and make sure that transfer of learning has taken place. They should also monitor training through the organization and measure the return of investment.

In summary, CPE practices of Provider B can be characterized by serving, promoting and fostering the work of their membership, conducting professional updates for their members, and having collaborative attempts with other professional bodies. The practice of managing and supervising CPE programs are minimum. Currently there is no policy on CPE; inexperience program planners run the programs, and resources and facilities are limited.

Provider C - Profile

Provider C was formed in 1959 as an affiliated body to the Institute for Chartered Secretaries and Administrators. Membership of the Institute is limited only to members and students of the Institute residing in Malaysia. At present the Institute has 4,700 members (comprising Fellows, Associates and Graduates) and 3,000 students.

There are two classes of membership at the Institute, i.e. Fellows and Associates. All qualified members of the Institute are entitled to describe themselves as Chartered Secretaries and use the designatory letters, FCIS or ACIS as appropriate. Fellowship is the senior grade of membership. Another grade, Grad ICSA comprises those who have successfully completed the examinations but have not yet gained sufficient qualifying service for Associateship.

In Malaysia, the Government has recognized this professional qualification as equivalent to honors degrees, recognizing the Fellow and Associate qualifications whilst the Graduate student is recognized as equivalent to a general degree. In tandem with its mission of developing good corporate professionals, Provider C is committed to maintaining the highest standard of integrity and ethical values within the profession. Provider C also acts as a change catalyst in the corporate arena, participating actively in the enhancement of corporate governance.

It has been championing best practices in corporate governance and educating the Malaysian corporate sector on its importance. It is the objective of Provider C to encourage and cultivate a continuing professional education culture amongst members to improve themselves and also to enhance the institution's image, status and dynamics of Provider C as the leading professional body for corporate secretaries and administrators in Malaysia. Provider C is being run as a business initiative with about twenty salaried staff. Members also elect a council consisting of a chairman and 12 council members to run the institute as a 'shadow cabinet, providing advice and direction.

The organization runs about 60 programs annually to improve and develop their members. Their institution is dynamic as their members are advisors to public listed companies, private limited companies in Malaysia. They also advise potential investors wanting to invest in our country.

Provider C - CPE Practices

Provider C organizes monthly CPE programmes for the benefit of members and the public. The programs are held in Kuala Lumpur, Penang, Johore Bahru, Kuching and Kota Kinabalu. Some of the activities conducted by Provider C are tea-talks, updates on the latest changes on company law, vocational trips for members, bilateral talks with the government sectors and business associations.

CPE points are allotted to a member who attends selected training sessions organized by the provider. The number of CPE points to be allotted will be dependent upon the duration of the session and will be stated in the program flyer. CPE points are offered to members who attend conferences, seminars, workshops and other related programs where information is disseminated and there is an opportunity to exchange views and opinions.

The objective of introducing the CPE point scheme is to encourage more participation from members of Provider C to take part in the training activities of the Association and that members are updated regularly on recent developments in their profession. In encouraging attendance by members to its training activities, the Association hopes that members would regard it as a positive and proactive move towards enhancement of the image, status and dynamism of the profession. The individual will determine the balance or mix of CPE hours that may be required. For members who are working in the Klang Valley, the minimum CPE points needed to renew their professional certificate are 30 CPE points, and those staying outside or in other states are required to clock in 15 CPE points for renewal. The CPE hours attained for each event will be indicated on the certificate of participation issued at the end of the event.

With effect from 1 January 2002, for every minimum CPE hours allotted for a calendar year, the member will be given a 50% discount. Members would need to produce their certificates of participation for all events attended to prove that he/she has achieved the minimum number of CPE points.

The profession itself has changed, being Chartered Secretaries; the Companies Commission of Malaysia, has revamped the laws relating to becoming company directors. The profession is enhanced with the role of advising the Board of Directors of public listed and non-listed company directors of their fiduciary duties.

This being the scenario, the profession has to play a major role as advisors to the board and the commission has introduced mandatory training programs to be attended by the directors before they can renew their directorship; and in this case the profession itself has to go through a metamorphosis. Members need to be more proactive and need to update their knowledge on technical and soft skills as company secretaries.

Currently, in this profession, CPE is non mandatory, but they are looking into making it one, *"because it is very important for our members to be continually updated, they need to be advised on legislation, regulation changes and the only way to updates these members would be through us, their professional body."*

Programs such as tea-talks, short two-day programs, seminars, workshops, conventions and forums are organized by the Provider at the center. This is to update members on topics that are non-company secretarial related. This is done to expose members to soft skills namely grooming, communication skills and dialogues with the relevant authorities, although there is no structured system to manage CPE. Brochures are sent to about 4,000 members and at least 50 percent of them respond and attend these programs. As for resources, the institution has a library and a small training room catering for tea-talks.

Financial resources are allocated for members to update themselves by the parent body in United Kingdom. Some of the programs are self-sustaining. Being a non-profit institution, profits are ploughed back to her members. Programs are monitored and evaluated through reaction sheets after each seminar. Comments from members are taken seriously for the running of future sessions.

Currently, there is no policy on CPE but the institution is looking into it. The ownership of CPE lies with the individual, being a professional. In this profession, if the member does not update himself or herself, they will have difficulties advising their clients on the latest changes in legislation and regulations. Therefore, the onus of CPE is with the individual. The institution, as a provider of training updates on current issues also sources out for speakers for their programs. At the same time, they also look into relevant topics recommended by their members.

With all these, members are pleased with the opportunities for updating. Members, who attend the updates, become knowledgeable with the latest issues and this enhances the return of investment for them. Programs are based on both generic and needs basis. Programs based on needs are directly related to the profession and the generic programs are management related topics. A committee who looks after all training matters manages the programs. Topics are identified, speakers are sourced, brochures are printed and their training assistant looks into the venues. All of these are done with the help of a training committee. The institution has collaborated to run either diploma programs or short seminars / workshops with University Malaya and University Utara Malaysia entitled Diploma in Corporate Governance and Company Secretarialship for their members as well as the public.

When comparing this profession with other professional bodies like the medical association, it is noted that in the medical profession they need to be updated on the latest issues because they are treating human beings whereas this is not the case here; but having said that the Provider does run about 60 programs annually, one a week to update members. The only difference here is it is not mandatory.

In summary, the CPE practices of Provider C can be characterized by recognition of a range of CPE activities, are encouraged to attend updates, needs of the programs are discussed with members and clients, an educational committee plans and administrates CPE programs and the cost of program updates, resources and facilities are subsidized by the parent company. There is no policy on CPE but the laws are changing to make it compulsory CPE evaluations are only at first level and there are collaborative attempts with other professional bodies.

Provider D - Profile

Provider D established herself as the voice for the real estate agents on May 3, 1989, to reflect a more professional image of the organization as it progresses through the years.

Presently, all practicing Estate Agents are required to be approved and registered with the Board of Valuers, Appraisers and Estate Agents in accordance with the Valuers, Appraisers and the Estate Agents Act 1981 as amended in 1984 to include Estate Agents. The Board of Valuers, Appraisers and Estate Agents is under the purview of the Ministry of Finance. Provider D has a membership of 1500 agents, out of which only about fifty percent are active agents. An elected President consisting of about 15 council members runs the institute.

The vision of the institute is to unite all her members in Malaysia and to keep up to date with the professional standard and code of ethics in the real estate field. Members are required to complete 10 CPE points before renewing their certificate of practice. Some of the activities conducted by the institute include tea-talks, update programs on the latest change in their vocation, conventions and vocation trips. Provider D is also affiliated to world bodies.

The industry went through a bad spate during the recession. Estate Agents either closed 'shop' or offered to join venture with their counterparts. Some left the trade to do other business whereas some sold their outfit and migrated. Presently, either agents are merging their business to cut down on overheads or go seek work with other estate agents.

Provider D - CPE Practices

The association has progressed very well in terms of running CPE programs over the last two years. It is emphasized that attendance for the program has increased and they have moved on to formulate the real estate negotiators course, which is a two full day program for new negotiators. With Provider D, CPE comes in different forms tea-talks, conventions, lunch talks and short seminars.

CPE is very important to the individual and the organization because, *"We realize that the rules, regulation, real estate property law, statutes, and the budgets are all very important to the profession, and we need to know what are the incentives provided by the government in relation to stamp duty exemptions and other exemptions. With changes taking place at the speed of light, members may miss the crucial point made by the relevant authorities."*

The organization collates all the pertinent information relating to the industry, analyzes and redistributes this information back to their members so that they are well informed of the latest issues. The organization needs to update it and the members because everything around the industry and profession are ever changing including the practice, behavior of consumers and the profession itself. From the organization's standpoint, they basically look at CPE as trying to keep everyone professional; as professional as they can be so that their image is upheld. There is no misrepresentation to the public. The real estate agent is supposed to be the guardian of the profession and therefore they should know what they are telling the public, and that is the latest and correct information

The programs of CPE in this organization range from technical to management related updates. Most of the CPEs are for the principal agents and employees of the agencies. Their role is always going back to their core objectives i.e. education, professionalism and keeping everyone updated with the latest changes. Accordingly, all principal agents must 'clock' in 10 CPE points annually to renew their certificate of practice. This is according to the changes to the real estate agents rules and regulation act by the Board of Valuers, Appraisers and Estate Agents 1986, which makes CPE mandatory for the estate agents.

Some of the roles played by the institution to advise or guide members on CPE are by calling them for tea-talks, conventions, and dialogues with relevant authorities. Committee meetings are also being held to keep the members informed of the next CPE programs being run. In addition to this, newsletters, brochures and websites are provided with the latest information on the CPE.

Members are also encouraged to attend by providing subsidized rates by the organization. Resources available by the organization consist of a rented floor in Petaling Jaya with a training room, a small library and some training aids. Bigger programs are held in hotels at subsidized rates to encourage more members to attend. Most of the programs are self-funded from the running of the various CPE programs. The organization too has 'well wishers' who sometimes donate or sponsor their programs thus underwriting all expenses.

Most of the times, CPE are monitored or evaluated through reaction sheets. In addition to this, during the seminars/workshops, attendance sheets are placed at the reception. Members need to sign-in and sign-out during the program. This discourages participants from signing in and only returning at the end of the day just to collect their CPE certificates. Furthermore, the reaction sheet is monitored and comments from the sheets are provided to the CPE chairman and committee, whereby the committee will report to the main committee for further action. Currently, there is no policy on CPE but there is a legislative requirement by the government to acquire 10 CPE points to renew their certificate of practice.

In this industry, ownership of CPE is market driven. If the programs are good, the members will attend and support the function or the program. Furthermore, the ruling by the Board on the industry mandates CPE ownership on the individual, but the organization and the consumers push for the enhancement of the latest knowledge on the industry.

The return on investment seen from attending these programs is quite promising. Members are more confident in advising clients, thus benefiting from the CPE programs.

Most of the programs run by the organization are based on both need and generic. Programs based on needs based are technical programs whereas generic programs are based on management related programs. Some of the programs organized are real estate negotiators program, conventions, tea / lunch talks, property related topics, feng shui and many others. The Vice President of Education and his committee manage the CPE calendar of activities on a voluntary basis. The committee recommends the programs for the year to the main council and after much deliberation; the council endorses the

CPE programs. The VP of Education together with the administrative and marketing staff designs, prints and markets the programs to the members. Sometimes the programs are advertised in the newspapers for the member's information.

The profession is governed by legislation, therefore making CPE mandatory. At the same time, estate agents will attend CPE programs if the program is market driven. Some of the members have clocked in more than 20-25 CPE points, higher than the required CPE points. This shows that members will attend if the programs are run with the members need in mind. The institution also collaborates with their international counterparts, the National Association of Realtors, USA to invite resource speakers. It also runs programs on a joint venture basis with the Board. The institution also has bi-lateral and collaborative understandings with related institutions in Japan, Indonesia, Australia and New Zealand.

In summary, the CPE practices of Provider D is characterized by CPE being compulsory for those practicing estate agency, recognizing a range of CPE activities, an employer of as a CPE coordinator and providing a well planned facility and resources. There are also collaborative attempts with similar professional bodies overseas. Evaluation is at first level but the programs run are kept up-to-date with business practices.

Provider E - Profile

Provider E is a leading management accountancy body which is recognized internationally for the high professional and technical standards of it's over 57,000 members, most of who work in industry, commerce or the public service. There are two grades of membership. Fellow (FCMA) and Associate (ACMA); the requirement being at least three years' practical experience for Fellowship at a more senior level than that required for Associateship. Being entirely self-financing, Provider E is an independent body. It is governed by a Council of Members whose work is supported by a number of standing committees and more than 300 permanent staff worldwide and at its headquarters in the UK.

In Malaysia, accredited members i.e. Associates and Fellows qualify for registration with the Malaysian Institute of Accountants. The Public Service Department recognizes the "Associate" accreditation as a professional qualification equivalent to an honors degree in accountancy awarded by local universities.

There are more than 74,000 students worldwide, of which 4,000 are in Malaysia. There are also more than 2,300 members locally. Provider E, a branch in Malaysia, consists of information, counseling and employment services, library and study facilities as well as owning branches, centers and networks. Provider E also produces their own newsletter as a channel of communication for their members. A dedicated CPE unit looks after the CPE of members through organizing programs such as evening talks, seminars and workshops on financial, management and topical issues. High profile events such as Lecture of the Year and CEO Forums are also held.

This institution is made up of members who are in the profession as management accountants.

Provider E - CPE Practices

Accordingly, business has been down with the recent financial crisis, which many companies are facing. Currently there is not much training done other than tea-talks, which is organized by other departments. In this context, the program is marketed internally to their members. These tea-talks are targeted towards their own members and students.

The institution caters for professional business accountants and runs long-term programs leading to a financial qualification in business. The current scenario is that with the changing markets and being in the business for more than twenty years, members need to update themselves with the latest developments centered on the business world, and therefore the respondent feels that training in terms of CPE is very important.

It is their belief that an individual should not think that education is redundant but should continue from womb to tomb. With globalization and change taking place, members should take the opportunity to update themselves.

Therefore CPE is important to both the individual and the institution. As for the institution, the stakeholders need to know what is happening around the business world, like the forums on WTO and AFTA. Assuming the members of the organization do not know the current issues pertaining to the business world, they will be left behind.

As for the individual, they could impart whatever knowledge, skill and attitude he has learnt in a positive learning environment thus putting to use whatever they have learnt. After all, learning is a lifelong learning process and getting ready for changes is imminent. The practice of CPE is very new in this institution and there is no system in the sense of recording and it was either kept by the Malaysia Institute of Accountants or the individual themselves. MIA has the authority to request members to update their knowledge.

As for the role-played in managing CPE, the institution designs, sources for the speakers, markets and delivers the programs to the members. For now, they are running short of manpower. The institution guides or advises the members on CPE through reminders, delivery of brochures and advising members on the benefits of attending the program. The institution has resources such as member-speakers, library, training aids and a small training room. Occasionally, they invite speakers from outside and programs on a bigger scale are held in hotels. Most of the CPE programs are run as low budget programs and are self- financing. This is the only way to attract members since they are still very young and as long as they break even and is of service to their own internal customers, they will continue to do so.

As for the evaluation of CPE programs, reaction sheets are sent to the participants and upon receiving, data are collected and analyzed, sending the feedback to the managers concerned and this is further taken to the council for action.

Currently, the institution has no policy on CPE. It is in the developmental stage and manpower is needed to manage the CPE department. As for the ownership of CPE, Provider E is of the view that the individual should own CPE because the individual should know what programs or updates he should go for. They believe that whatever you have learned stays with you and what you have to take out to the organization is you putting it into practice. This also allows the return on investment on the institution because the member has just contributed towards the latest knowledge needed for the organization.

The CPE programs are mostly run on a needs basis for the member profession. There is no big scale plans now to run CPE programs as the institution is still in its formative stage. Given another three years, they ought to be ready to develop more CPE programs. Currently, apart from tea-talks, there is not much CPE in action. An education committee who is responsible to identify relevant topics, source speakers, and design and deliver the programs to the members manages the programs. During the program, the department records the attendance of the participants and the number of hours attended .The institution also undertakes to collaborate with the Malaysia Employers' Group to improve the provision and methods of training and evaluation for their students and also jointly to provide job opportunities with JobStreet.com.

In summary, the CPE practices of Provider E are characterized by an obligatory CPE policy, providing advice and consultancy to members, conducts a range of CPE activities recognized for re-licensure, has an education committee who plans and administrates the programs, and collaboration with other professional bodies.

Provider F - Profile

Provider F makes up for the accounting fraternity and has been recognized and respected across the world for almost 100 years, and currently has nearly 300,000 students and members in 160 countries. Whatever the background, Respondent F addresses the individual needs and goals on an ongoing partnership, which is designed to last throughout their career.

Lifelong learning continues beyond membership through their portfolio of continuing professional education opportunities, including a bespoke MBA and a range of additional diplomas and certificates.

Provider F's programs are designed to meet the skills and training demands at various levels across different industries. For this purpose, Provider F will be collaborating with professional bodies and training providers such as I-Mesdaq

Sdn Bhd, Malaysian Institute of Taxation (MIT), Institut Bank-Bank Malaysia (IBBM), Malaysian Institute of Management (MIM) and the British Council.

The institution consists of 12,000 members, inclusive of students. This division was set-up in Malaysia, where the head office being in England. The office is situated on the 27th floor in the heart of the city, providing a bird's eye view of the city.

Over the past few years the organization has run more than sixty short programs for their members, mostly tea-talks. These short programs are accredited with 3 CPE points. The current business scenario after the 9/11 incidents had much impact on the business performance. As most of the organization's members are certified chartered accountants, they have to advise their clients on the recent and impending changes after the 9/11 incidents and the Asian financial crisis. Thus, attending CPE programs were the last things on their minds. The institution is coming up with new strategies to take the organization to the forefront.

Provider F - CPE Practices

CPE is very important to the organization because it is a professional organization consisting of accountants. They need to constantly update themselves in terms of their experiences and update on the latest issues by the relevant bodies. Moreover, CPE points are required for the upgrading of the individuals professional membership. To be eligible for the status of Fellowship, a member must fulfill the required 35-CPE points per year for 3 consecutive years. If a member does not want to upgrade him or herself, their upgrading will be delayed for 3 to 6 years for the next upgrade. Thus, the advice or guidance from the organization is that they encourage the members to be an 'all rounded person', as this is part of professional education.

In this context, advice and guidance is given to members not only to attend programs on auditing, taxation or accounting but also on soft skills programs like communication skills, team building, and presentation skills, to name a few. The members very well receive the programs. Added to this the resources allocated to the institution for CPE purposes includes a library with relevant books and magazines, training rooms, students room, pantry and a computer room where members can surf the net. Locally, the organization does not have a technical department but the main office in UK has one, whereby members can conduct research. The resource also includes a comprehensive website for their members' convenience. Resource speakers are available from their own membership.

On financial support for CPE, programs are run on a self-financing or on a break-even basis. For major events like conventions and forums, the organization invites external sponsors to underwrite. The main office in UK looks into budgeting or underwrites CPE programs on a case-to-case basis. As for a system of monitoring on CPE programs, only reaction sheets are given to the participants and collected, thereafter analyzed and feedback provided to the membership manager. This is then taken to the council for further discussion if there are any issues.

There is no policy for CPE but this is done through encouragement and the individual's will to be a self-directed learner. Furthermore the member is self-motivated to upgrade their membership, which is a requirement by the organization. The ownership of CPE is by two parties, i.e., the providers and the individual.

The organization will definitely continue to encourage their members to do it, because they do see the importance of such professional development courses, but the catch is that without the realization from the individual, there is nothing much that they could do. They are bound to try their best but still, the effort has to come from the members. If they are really willing to update and upgrade themselves, then they will attend.

The return on investment from running the CPE programs for the members are seen in the form of members enhancing themselves professionally with their clients and fellow members. Other than members themselves measuring the return on investment, ROI is intangible here.

The organization runs CPE programs based on needs and generic. Some of the programs run on a needs basis include taxation, auditing, accounting, national budgets, especially during budget presentation, updating on the latest rules and regulation to members while the generic programs are based on soft skills such as communication, presentation skills, team development, and management development programs.

Most of the CPE programs are co-coordinated by a training co-coordinator. The programs are developed initially through a need analysis and when topics and speakers are confirmed, this then goes for approval by the education committee and thereafter by the main council. The CPE programs are then printed, and posted to all the members, consisting of 12,000 individual persons. The programs are also marketed through newsletters, website and tele-calls.

In comparison to other professional bodies that have made CPE either compulsory or mandatory, this institution is governed by the rules and regulation of the Malaysian Institute of Accountants. All accountants are required to register themselves with this body to practice the business. Therefore, even though they are a division that is currently being set up in the country, they do not want to duplicate things. MIA is the current regulator of all the accountants in Malaysia. They have very strict policies on this and Provider F has decided to leave this to them.

On the issue of collaboration, the institution does collaborate with other similar organizations such as the Malaysian Institute of Accountants, the Malaysian Investment Association, Public Universities and other professional bodies. The institution also conducts joint venture programs with government initiatives agencies like small and medium size industries. To further develop their members' soft skills, the institution has initiated the setting up of a Toastmasters Club, to develop public speaking skills for the members.

One of the main challenges faced by the institution is that there are too many accounting bodies representing the profession, namely the Chartered Public Accountants, Australia; the Chartered Institute of Management Accountant, UK, to name a few. All these bodies run various CPE programs directly competing with each other and there are many programs, which are duplicated, and members then compare the prices and these arises conflicts amongst the providers. Provider F is trying to cut down on the oversupply of training programs and trying to find collaborators in order to solve this issue.

In summary, the CPE practices of Provider F are characterized by providing guidance and advice to members, conducting a range of CPE activities and allocating ample resources and facilities for members to update themselves. There is no policy on CPE and therefore it is not compulsory. Program planners and administrators are made up of committee members. Collaboration with other similar bodies is evident.

Provider G - Profile

Provider G is a public university about 70 years in existence and dedicated to the ideals of lifelong education. She also offers numerous programs to the working adults to acquire additional knowledge and skills related to their vocation for career advancement. Provider G is also an extension school, namely continuing education, to a public university. Professional programs offered at Provider G include in-house training as well as certificate and diploma courses. Course participants will have excellent opportunities to enhance and enrich their knowledge and skills, and to benefit from the vast database of resources and expertise available at the University. All programs are designed to meet the needs of rapidly developing Malaysia, providing it with a definite competitive edge by having well-trained workers. Since its establishment, Provider G has trained about 4,900 students in numerous programs at certificate and diploma levels.

As a center of extension at the university, Provider G is able to undertake quality programs given the wide and varied academic resources available. Well-qualified lecturers and very experienced practitioners conduct classes to ensure that what is imparted is relevant and practical. Classes are usually held in the evenings or during weekends for the convenience of students. Teaching methodology is varied; from lectures to seminars, workshops, case studies and multimedia presentations to facilitate effective learning.

Provider G's objective is to provide quality training and educational programs to meet the ever-changing needs of society through knowledgeable and skilled work force in the context of lifelong education. Furthermore, the institution is to continuously review and update all curricula and materials used for the various programmes and to keep up to date with current trends. Provider G is to develop the culture of learning among working adults to better cope with the challenges of globalization.

All curricula and teaching materials are developed under the supervision of well-qualified lecturers and practitioners in the respective fields. The continuous interaction between the academics and the professionals provides invaluable input to all programs developed and implemented by the institution. The programs that are conducted by Provider G are:

- Executive Diploma in Human Resource Management
- Executive Diploma in Management
- Professional Diploma in Early Childhood Education (UM)
- Executive Diploma in Accounting Administration
- Executive Diploma in Information Technology
- Certificate in Early Childhood Education
- Certificate Course in Malay Language Proficiency
- Certificate Course in English Language Proficiency

Provider G is an extension school of a public university, and is being run by a Director for the center of continuing education. A staff strength of 30 supports the center.

The institution is the oldest public university in Malaysia. Recently it has branched out to provide evening or part-time programs to participants, who are adult learners. The division is part of the center for continuing education.

The institution has gone through some business change during the recent Asian financial crises and the 9/11 incidents. As such the University took a change to cater for the adult learner who had to make decisions whether to continue their studies locally or overseas. With this in mind, the branch was set-up to cater for the adult learners. With the ongoing recession, many private companies wanted to send their employees for further training to enhance their skills and catering for working adults, looking for an avenue to continue their studies. The financial crisis played in the organization's favor whereby neighboring countries like Thailand, Bangladesh, and Pakistan to name a few sent their public officers for training at the center for continuing education.

Provider G - CPE Practices

The institution sees the importance on CPE because it carries the brand name and should change accordingly to business situations. Business climate is dynamic therefore the organization is ready to meet the challenges of the business world. As for the individual, CPE is very important because the individual needs to update himself with current knowledge and skills and attitude, and with the recent incidents that have taken the whole world by surprise, many individuals need to be multi-skilled and self-directed learners.

The institution has embarked on a total quality management program for its employees, added with pep talks to boost employee's morale. The institution also sends its employees to private training providers to attend short courses to update themselves. The center plays the role of CPE provider and updates of short-term programs ranging from 2-24weeks.

Upon completing these short-term programs, a certificate or a diploma is awarded for participants to progress to further a degree program. It also manages latest updates for the parent organization. It also plays the role of an investigator of policies and studies what is needed in the market so that it can provide what the market needs.

The center also advises and guides employers association on the latest trends in the business world thus requesting the employers to send their employees to update themselves to face future challenges. This is made through addressing and presenting conference papers, seminars and conducting previews for the working adults and employer associations.

The center provides a wide variety of resources. The library is equipped with the latest books, computer rooms, training rooms, lecture theatres and a canteen. It also provides support staff to handle enquiries from the participants or students. The CPE programs are run on budgets allocated by the center.

Retreats are self-financed. The programs conducted by private consultants are paid on a per-day rate. Since this center is government funded, there are monies allocated for CPE programs that run at a lost because it is being sponsored.

The CPE programs are evaluated through examinations, assignments, and attendance at each level of the participant's attendance at the center. Lecturers and the program are evaluated with reactions sheets given to participants and feedback to the Senior Manager if there are any pressing issues.

Currently there is no policy on CPE at the center. It is more a norm and an essential tool, which needs to be there. It is also a challenge because it is not easy to introduce a policy whereby there are many resistances to it, and monitoring becomes a burden. Ownership of CPE should be with the organization and the individual. The organization keeps a tab on the business conditions and their strategy to reach the organizational goals and the individual needs to own it in line with the development of the individual to contribute towards the role theory. ROI is enhanced through employee improvement, morale, productivity and promotions, which also contributes towards staff pinching from the competitors.

The CPE programs that are conducted at the center are diploma in human resources management, information technology, certificate in early childhood, and accounting. Most of these programs are based on a generic basis; but recently, the center has been looking at providing specific programs to cater to the needs of the working adult. Program development is managed through a program development management unit, where quality is looked into.

This is culminated through weekly meetings and monitoring of the programs. The center affirms that the individual needs to update oneself constantly in this volatile business condition. The center also collaborates with other private university-colleges in other fields like information technology, accounting and corporate governance.

In summary the CPE practices of provider G is characterized by encouraging and fostering better relationship among their colleagues, availability of ample resources and facilities, encouraging updates and knowledge reviews, paper presentations, and encouraging collaborative work with other universities and independent consultancies. There is no policy on CPE and is not compulsory. A program-planning unit manages program planning and development. Evaluation is seen as a tedious task and usually is at first level only.

Provider H - Profile

Provider H is a public university and is at the centre for graduate studies. She takes pride in being one of the premier institutions of higher education in Malaysia. The history of Provider H dates back to 1956, but the genesis and growth of the Centre for Graduate Studies (CGS) can be traced to April 1997.

Prior to this, graduate education programs at Provider H was carried out in collaboration with a number of foreign universities, namely:

- Executive Masters of Business Administration with Ohio University, USA
- Masters of Business Administration with Cardiff, UK
- Masters in Arts Education with De Montfort, UK
- Masters in Accountancy with Curtin University, Australia
- Masters in Mass Communication with Ohio State University, USA
- Masters in Sports Science with University of New South Wales, Australia

According to the annual report sighted, it was the passing and ratification of the Higher Education Act in 1966 that laid the foundation of the establishment of center for graduate studies (CGS). Although relatively new, the Centre prides itself as being progressive, dynamic and innovative in fulfilling its aims of providing opportunities for Bumiputra graduates to further their education at masters and doctoral levels.

This endorses its vision of engendering academic excellence and being in the forefront of graduate academic advancement. In striving to raise the levels of professional graduate education, it is the centre's mission to nurture the creation of a graduate learning community by providing educational opportunities that would help to push its frontiers in achieving national aspirations.

Center for Graduates Studies (CGS) operates as the nerve-centre of graduate-level education within the university and is responsible for the implementation and management of the overall administration of postgraduate studies. It coordinates and formulates policies on admission and academic regulations as well as provides support to facilitate research and learning among graduate students.

A Director of Graduate School runs the center with full time employees, managing the various programs that are being run by the university. The institution is situated at Shah Alam, Selangor. It started off as a government funded Institution of Higher Learning and was upgraded recently to the status of a University by the Ministry of Education.

The institution encourages the private sector to consult the faculty or unit heads on the projects undertaken by the company. The expertise from the unit head is sought either to collaborate or just provide consultancy services for a fee. These units may provide consultancy services or undertake turnkey projects.

This is to encourage the academic staff to provide the expertise sought and gain experience from the project undertaken from a business organization's view. These projects are on going for a number of years and they include interior designing, accounting and hospitality management.

It is revealed that Provider G is responsible for the nation's skills development program, especially for the Bumiputras. Respondent G, together with the government's initiative, has collaborated with developed nations to set-up skill development schools in Malaysia. As such Provider G has collaborated with the French, German, Spain and the Japanese to set up these skill development centers.

These centers train school leavers who would like to develop a skill such as arching, welding, motor mechanics, engineering, plumbing, mechanical engineering, and lathe work. Some of the graduates are quickly absorbed into government bodies and the private sectors. Currently about 10,000 students are studying at these centers.

Provider H - CPE Practices

It is surprising to note that what is very clear is the employers are very interested in upgrading their people and staff to compete in the competitive business environment, but many employers are perhaps not too clear on how the upgrading can be achieved and what are the areas needed to do so. Therefore, more often than not, they do come and vaguely request for training without knowing precisely what they want. Their ability to analyze the need of their own business is limited. As far as the individuals who are working at the moment is very clear that the lifelong employment concept is now at the doldrums. People have to look after themselves. The concept of being loyal to the organization has gone out. Loyalty is no longer an issue. It's employability.

On the same note, many employees are feeling unsure with regards to their job, especially with major institutions downsizing and terminating their employees, closing down operations and relocating to other countries. The employees are responsible for their employability because they have not updated themselves with the current knowledge and skills required for the business and thus, are blaming the employer for not providing training. When asked what they have done for themselves with regards to learning and development, their usual reply is always that they are waiting for the institution to send them for updates.

On the context of whether CPE is important to the individual and the institution, the centre emphasizes that CPE is very essential. The fact that the knowledge base needed by the worker is changing so fast, people become out-of date by the time they graduate from any form of program. Both the institution and the individual should be constantly updating themselves with new information and they are indeed doing so but ironically, most learning is not used and transferred to the workplace.

The running of CPE programs is prominent in the institution. It is a convention that the academic staff is required to update themselves constantly pertaining to their subject matter. It is the organization's philosophy that the academic staff attends various relevant programs at least once every year. Some of the CPE programs are very expensive and occasionally, in specialized fields. Others include conferences seminars and forums that are mainly held overseas.

Some academic staff that are not interested in their own development are encouraged to attend to update, but then again there are always other ways to develop oneself and ones knowledge without attending external events. This can be done through reading the latest journals and relevant books on one's particular academic expertise and acquire enough knowledge through that. There is a belief that to a certain extent a learning event is rewarding and enriching.

Currently, the institution does not have a CPE system in place, but this is slowly changing to accommodate a system. There is also no compulsion in attending the CPE programs by the individual, only in the instances of student complains with regards to 'old' knowledge disseminated by the individual. When this happened, the individual is required to go in for a counseling session to look into individual development.

In this instance, the organization plays a role in organizing relevant CPE programs to update the individuals. These programs are offered internally and conducted by senior academic staff, who may be brought in from overseas or by a local facilitator, which is directly related to the individuals' field. These CPE programs are also open to the public and the private sector. The organization provides very little advice or guidance in relation to the individual CPE, as this is the role of the Dean of the faculty. This role will be played during the process of performance appraisal; however it will not be brought up if there are no issues. Some deans of faculties may take their own initiatives to conduct meetings with their academic staff to identify their needs and encourage them to update themselves; but this process is very rare.

These are some of the frustrations that the organization is facing at the moment. There are no structures and systems in place whereby the organization could identify the academic needs of the employees. Currently, the centre is so focused on the students' need that there is no one looking into the internal needs of the academic staff. They are in the process of discussing this and coming up with ways on how they could look into helping the academic staff, especially now as they are moving into a knowledge economy and with the competition from the private universities and among public universities.

The goal of the institution is to produce graduates who will be successful and functional in the job market. To ensure this, the academic staff need to be knowledgeable and as such, the institution is exploring ideas on how to ensure that this will be carried out.

The institution has identified two types of resources. The first being financial, whereby a very large budget is set aside for the academic staff to attend CPE programs internally or externally. The second being physical resources, journals, CD-ROMs, computer labs, library, lecture rooms, training aids and other relevant reading materials. Financial support or fund allocation is given by the government. The budgets are large but sometimes not enough for the fast growing organization. The institution has over a dozen city and state campuses and occasionally, resources are overlapped and wastage takes place.

The financial allocations are also for the updating and development of the academic staff. Some are provided scholarships to complete their post-graduate studies in the US, UK and Australia. The institution does not have a monitoring and evaluation system. Individuals are supposed to report back to the head of unit and share the experiences with their colleagues. There is no formal system or a written policy. The onus of reporting is with the individual and sometimes it becomes a sensitive issue. Moreover, the CPE programs and events have no link with their performance appraisal.

The institution has no policy on CPE. They are only looking into it currently with the recent call by the various bodies for K-economy. As for the ownership of the CPE, the institution provides the resources, sets the policy and monitors the progress of the learner and the provider. The individual will need to choose the relevant learning programs to cater to his/her learning needs and the provider has to look into the institution and the individual's learning and development goals and needs.

The institution does not have a system to monitor the return on investment. There are also no attempts to analyze data on the investment made on CPE or updates. Moreover, the data is considered confidential and tricky because the organization is a non-profit making body.

On the other hand, the organization encourages academic staff in some faculty to provide consultancy service work on a short-term basis or on a project-to-project basis. This is to keep in touch with whatever the individual has learnt and encouraging a transfer of learning that takes place at every stage during the consultancy. Even by providing this consultancy work, the institution finds it difficult to calculate the return on investment since there is no direct advantage to the university and it is left to the good faith of the individual to provide feedback.

Some of the challenges faced by the institution with regards to CPE are developing a system to facilitate CPE. Some employees may take advantage of the system and upgrade themselves, while others will not.

The institution lacks a system and the recognition of the importance of putting a system in place. The budget and the resources are provided with a certain constraint and everybody wants a part of this small budget. Since there is a lack of system to monitor the CPE development, the individual may take advantage of the system to attend more CPE programs and this brings about conflict in the organization.

As discussed earlier, the individual takes the initiative to seek the required CPE updates and apply for the allocation of budgets through the unit head, and further approved by the faculty head. Upon their approval, the candidates go for the updates. At this stage, it must be emphasized that the onus of updating lay solely on the individual and he/she must take the initiative to find out how the current system works. There is nobody who is going to sit down and explain how the system works. The challenge here is developing and putting the system in its place whereby everybody has a fair chance to apply for the CPE programs.

The other challenges faced by the institution are the sensitivity of CPE development. Some individuals have barriers, such as issues with ego whereby they think that they know it all. Thus, by attending CPE programs, they feel embarrassed and belittled, not knowing that they need to update themselves as they climb the ladder of success.

Some of the events related to CPE that are conducted or encouraged to attend are conventions, seminars and workshops, forums, dialogues and long-term post graduates programs directly related to their field. Most of the programs are based on a need. Staff that needs to update themselves on their soft skills attends the generic programs.

In this program the lecturers provide the latest input to the participants on academic theory and bring back experiences shared by the participants who have been in the industry for a very long time. This mix provides enrichment to both participants and the academic staff.

On the other hand, the Pusat Pengajaran manages CPE programs and these programs are based on a need. This unit only provides teaching methodologies and technologies on a regular basis. There are full time staffs that just facilitate these programs on a regular basis. Currently, there is no collaborative attempt to conduct programs on a joint venture basis. The organization had a collaborative program two decades ago, whereby the organization had sent two teams of academic staff to understudy the program in the United States, but now the organization conducts the program on their own. Furthermore, there is no written rule on collaboration and policy. Therefore it is very rare for this provider to collaborate.

On the comparison between other professional bodies like the medical or the engineering profession, the centre feels that their profession deals with life and death and where medicine and engineering is legislated, theirs is not. At the same time the business industry feels that there is no need to go for regular updates and there seems to be a strong resistance to anything that is being introduced from overseas. The business profession does not want to experiment or rock the boat since the local environment provides no challenge to the profession, especially the HR profession.

The HR personnel themselves are afraid to experiment new things; it is their personal fear. Experiment means failure and they cannot take failure. There are many ideas that work and some may fail and they have to share these experiences with their fellow professionals.

Young people now have got a very different picture on what they want and are willing to look for. They are not afraid to quit their jobs and to go elsewhere looking for their dreams. If the centre doesn't provide them with conduciveness in working environment that satisfies their needs, the whole country is going to have a productivity problem because too much turnover is bad for the country. Therefore the profession itself should update themselves with the latest CPE updates so that they in turn could provide some inputs to the yuppie generation of learners.

Moreover, it is the respondent's observation that the profession is allowing anybody to practice without a bona-fide certification. Therefore, there must be a system of certification whereby the individual has to undergo the process of certification and only then, the profession will be looked up to.

In summary, the CPE practices of Provider H is characterized by a philosophy on CPE and learning, the guidance and advise provided by the dean of the faculty, acknowledgements in the importance of CPE updates and programs, allocation of ample financial resources and facilities to encourage learning, planning and managing CPE programs through an education committee and encouraging collaborative activities with other universities and professional bodies.

Provider I - Profile

Provider I is the region's first private MSC-Status virtual university where education is delivered through the pervasive use of e-learning technology such as the Internet, web-based or CD-based courseware and facilitator-based tutorials or academic meetings.

Provider I started its operation on 18 December 1997 when it received the invitation letter to set up a university from the Minister of Education, the Honourable Dato' Sri Mohd Najib Tun Abdul Razak. The Minister launched the university on 21 December 1998 at Kelana Jaya Study Centre. Subsequently, it received its establishment letter in February 1999 from the Ministry of Education. The Ministry of Education approved the registration of Provider I on 28 January 2000. Provider I received the MSC Status on 10 September 2001, the certificate of which was presented by the Prime Minister of Malaysia, Dato Seri Dr. Mahathir bin Mohamed on 22nd June 2002.

Provider I is wholly owned by KUB Malaysia Berhad, a Bumiputera public-listed company on the main board of the Kuala Lumpur Stock Exchange (KLSE). Provider I to-date offers 18 academic programmes in the field of Business Administration, Information Technology, Humanities and Social Science. Both the Jabatan Pelajaran Selangor (JPS) and the National Accreditation Council (LAN) have approved these programmes. Provider I has registered more than 8000 students at 8 study centers in Malaysia, and 1 in Cambodia. Provider I's, programs are going to be offered in Thailand, Indonesia and the

Middle East as part of its global expansion. Provider I has also received national accreditation for 9 of its 18 programs. Provider I's students are also eligible to apply for education loans available from both government and private bodies. Provider I is a private organization and being run as a profit center. The employees are retired professors and experienced academic staff. The Director of the institute reports to the board of directors.

The institution is a private university based in Petaling Jaya, operating from a row of rented shop lots. The university provides undergraduate programs for the public. The center is part of the Ministry of Education and has emerged as the national and international leader in educational leadership.

Provider I - CPE Practices

The institution strongly believes in CPE and development by the institution and the individual. It introduced the concept of letterheads carrying a motto along the lines of 'knowledge development, people development and institution development' and is also a firm believer of lifelong learning that takes place happens anytime and anywhere.

Using models from United Kingdom and Singapore the institution has prepared a proposal for the then ministry of education and had got it approved, saying that every teacher should have approximately one month or 150 hours of training. Meetings are also seen as CPE practices and it is argued that meetings are not just routine meetings or administrative meetings but development meetings and process of learning and these are where learners can benefit if they build a common linguistic structure among staff that everything the institution does is a learning process.

The institution encourages the practice of CPE through the transfer of learning at both private and public sectors. Staffs are encouraged to attend CPE programs for about 150 hours and upon their return they are supposed to share their ideas with other colleagues. The institution also encourages the academic staffs to prepare research papers and co-present them nationally or internationally. Staffs are invited to attend the courses and create opportunities for them to practice and learn. The institution's role in managing CPE is through the respondent requesting for photocopies of the programs attended and/or papers presented. These are further distributed to other academic staffs for their reading purposes. The presenters are also encouraged to write reviews about their experiences and share them with their colleagues.

The institution also provides guidance and advice based on two notions: educability and trainability. They invite everybody to see beyond the notion that learning is borderless and review the distinction between formal, non-formal and informal learning. As for the second notion they emphasize that knowledge is expending exponentially, which includes data and information that becomes obsolete very fast. The need for self-renewal and the updating of competency builds the self- confidence and self respect which is tied up to the capacity to learn and to master what the learner wants to do.

The institution's belief is that one should not spare any expenses in developing the human resources of the institution. Education is an investment and training too is an investment and therefore adequate funding is important to have the highest level of learning. Other resources are readily available, i.e. libraries, computer labs, training aids, training rooms, and canteens. As for financial supports the private sector's bureaucracy and red tape hinders the progress. The need for approval depends on the policy of the organization and need to be sanctioned by the Chief Executive Officer.

As for the system of monitoring and evaluation, the institution practices the government system of monitoring. Upon returning from the CPE update, the participant provides a report to the Head of Department and after 6 months, re-evaluates the outcomes with the individuals. Sometimes this can be tricky because the job or the learning outcome may look good during the training event but when it comes to implementation, other factors maybe taken into consideration. The organization uses the performance management system as the tool for evaluation. As this organization is a profit making body, each individual is answerable to the faculty heads or the unit heads. This is because there is no policy on CPE practices and this is done on an ad-hoc basis; as and when it is required by the organization.

All parties concerned should negotiate the ownership of CPE practices. There must be matching of interest by all parties concerned; that is, generic skills, specialized skills or personal interest. As such all parties may gain if the ownership is negotiated. Furthermore the return on investment is seen clearly from the confidence of the person to enable his job in a better capacity. These return on investment are intangible and spills over into other domains of life. The return on investment, which is tangible, can be seen through the transfer of the learning technology at the workplace.

The institution conducts programs on professional and skill development, management development, technical oriented programs and change management programs. These programs are based both on need and generic base, depending on the organization, individuals and the provider. Programs are close matched between the organization and the individual. Programs are managed in an elaborate way because of national consumption.

The programs are managed from around the world with best practices and education committees that manage program development. In this context, the institution wanted to set up a national qualification for the headmasters. As early as 1993, the institution has been sending participants for the related program to US, England and Canada to conceptualize the framework for the program. After much work, the master framework was established for the headmasters.

This shows that program development is managed seriously in this organization. At the organization, CPE programs are carried out on a want basis. There is the gap, which is being closed between the rich and the poor, and there is easy excess to information towards CPE programs. This is based on the organization being a private and profit center and participants gain easy access to the Internet.

On the notion that the medical profession is more CPE prone, the institution sees it as a matter of life and death. In such professions as medical, engineering and law, they are considered to be pure profession. The body of knowledge and skills needed in these professions are very dynamic when compared to other professions like human resource, teaching or accounting. In comparison to the former, the body of knowledge changes every 6 months and the latter only after 2 to 3 years. A constant update is definitely needed. Having said that, the institute also encourages other professions to emulate these pure professions and update themselves before the move to legislate them.

During the heydays, collaboration attempts were made with other education centers around the world through the Ministry of Education. Many prominent educationist, educational leadership officers and professionals in other areas are brought in to Malaysia to help contribute to the development of the education center.

Currently the ideals to collaborate are there, but are sorely depending on the various faculties and the interest they have. Some of the challenges faced by the professional bodies as seen by the respondent are quite challenging. The first seems to be the challenge of leadership and having a vision. Many leaders want to have power and to control territory. They have to decide whether to be a local player or go global. There is a need to look into resources, be it financial or physical resources.

Another challenge is that the laws has not been updated to regularize the professional bodies since most of these professional bodies come under the registrar of societies act, and run their organization as a society. These organizations need to put their house in order and decide where they would want to go and what and how they want to contribute to their members and if in the long run the members are disappointed with the organization, then they will resign and the organization dies naturally.

In summary, the CPE practices of Provider I is characterized by the guidance, advise and encouragement by the dean of the respective faculty, paper presentation at conventions and conferences, contribution to journal articles, programs planned and managed by an experienced committee and collaborative activities encouraged with professional bodies. There is no policy on CPE and evaluation is seen as a tedious task.

CHAPTER 8

CONTEXTUAL FACTORS ASSOCIATED WITH CPE PRACTICES

Institutional settings may vary in size, complexity and purpose but they have something in common. The institutional context is a major determinant of the understanding of effective practice. CPE practices to a large extent are influenced by the context in which they are practiced. In this context, data analysis shows that there are contextual factors that are associated with CPE practices in the various institutions.

Patton (1990) points out that multiple sources of information are sought and used because no single source of information can be trusted to provide a comprehensive perspective. By using a combination of observations, interviewing and document analysis, and the fieldworker is able to use different data sources to validate and crosscheck findings. Four categories of contextual factors were identified, and these factors are associated with CPE practices in all the providers. The factors are displayed in Table 2. They are: Importance of CPE, Ownership of CPE, Planning CPE updates, and CPE practices of collaborative relationships. All these factors are interrelated and they do not construe in any order of importance. The above contextual factors will be discussed in detail, together with relevant opinions and observations that will be quoted to provide insight.

Firestone (1987) reviews the qualitative study as telling quotes from interviews, a describing of agency and staffing patterns, and excerpts from agency history where the details are convincing because they create a picture that make sense to the reader. The contextual factors are presented below with an explanation on how they are associated with CPE practices of selected professional providers in Malaysia.

Table 2: Contextual Factors Associated With CPE Practices

CPE Practices

Provider	Philosophy of CPE	Professional Functions	Program Planning & Development	Program Administration & Evaluation
A	Importance of CPE	Advise/ guidance, ownership of CPE	Need basis /CPE planning model	Resources, budget & facilities; administration, collaboration
B	Policy of CPE	Advise/ guidance, ownership of CPE	Update of CPE, related CPE programs	Resources, budget & facilities; administration, collaboration
C	Importance of CPE, ownership of CPE	Advise/ guidance, managing CPE	Update of CPE, need basis/ CPE planning model	Resources, budget & facilities; administration, collaboration
D	Policy of CPE, importance of CPE, ownership of CPE	Advise/ guidance, managing CPE	Update of CPE, need basis/ CPE planning model	Resources, budget & facilities; collaboration
E	Importance of CPE	Advise/ guidance, ownership of CPE	Update of CPE, related CPE programs, need basis/ CPE planning model	Resources, budget & facilities; administration, collaboration
F	Importance of CPE	Ownership of CPE, managing CPE	Update of CPE, related CPE programs	Resources, budget & facilities; administration, collaboration

G	Importance of CPE	Advise/ guidance, managing CPE	Related CPE programs, need basis/ CPE planning model	Resources, budget & facilities; administration, collaboration
H	Importance of CPE	Ownership of CPE, managing CPE	Related CPE programs, need basis/ CPE planning model	Resources, budget & facilities; administration
I	Policy of CPE, importance of CPE	None	Update of CPE, related CPE programs, need basis/ CPE planning model	Resources, budget & facilities; administration, collaboration

Importance of CPE

The first contextual factor indicates the importance of CPE to the individual, the provider and the organization. This factor is given prominence throughout most organizational literature. Most of the times, these are reflected in their mission statements, goals or objectives and the members are encouraged, guided, and or advised to attend CPE programs.

Institutions, in order to keep up with change, are developing their members and clients in new knowledge, skills and innovation to keep up with the rapidly changing work environment. Professional members, providers and the various institutions realize that they need to respond quickly to changing market conditions, meet client requirements and government policies. As such both the members and the organization realize that keeping up-to-date is central to the professional and the organization.

Provider A agrees that CPE is important to the members and the organization. They believe that the institution needs to update their members and employees in the latest products, skills and technologies so that they can be very competitive. At the same time, the individuals need to refresh themselves to understand what changes are taking place in their environment and whether they can now adapt to these new changes. Provider B, on the other hand, deems that it's a matter of survival. One needs to update oneself professionally.

Learning is life-long. Lifelong means institution have to also cater for people who have stopped working or retired, because they too have to learn to adapt themselves to the new activities, changing environment. There could be a lot of these development opportunities offered to them with an abundance of different certifications and relevant updates. The response from Provider C to this factor is that CPE is relevant but not mandatory, and the provider is looking into making it mandatory.

Members need to be continually updated, they have to be advised on any legislature changes, regulation changes and the only way a lot of the members can get these changes is through the professional body. Provider D looks at this factor as very crucial because their members are accountable to the public. Provider D understands that the rules and regulations of the real estate, property law, statutes and the announcement of the national budget in the parliament are dynamic to their industry. As such, they need to update their members the soonest possible.

This industry thrives on the economic changes and looks forward to government incentives from stamp duty to exemption of property gains tax. This institution collates all relevant information pertaining to the above, analyses and concise them before sending it to their members. The institution emphasizes that:

> "…everything around us is vibrant and changing, in line with the practice itself, the behavior of people, the behavior of consumers changes in the business; therefore there is a need for forums, workshops so that the practitioner can exchange notes on the changes taking place in the practice which is required so that we keep ourselves updated with human behavior and law in any instance"

They further expounded that:

> "…from the provider's standpoint I think basically, we look at CPE as trying to keep everyone professional, as professional

as they can be so that the image is upheld and there is no misrepresentation to any parties. The real estate agent are suppose to be guardian of the profession and therefore they should know what they are telling the public; the latest and correct information."

Provider E sees this factor as very important because they are business advisers. The current market, which is volatile, needs sharp decisions to be made and members of this institution need to have them. According to Provider E, the organization needs to know what is happening around the business world, what is the latest development in the financial sector, the impact of AFTA and NAFTA and changes at the world trade organization.

The respondent sees the relationship between the organization and the individual as a partnership. When the institution invests in the individual's CPE, the individual puts in practice the knowledge gained at the updates by advising the client on the latest development in the business sector. As such, the institution gains through the investment made on CPE updates for the individual.

The institution also notes the importance of this factor to the individual. They see the importance of CPE as, "a learning process from womb to tomb", a lifelong process. The institution also looks at the current business scenario and suggests that since organizations are looking at multi-tasking, multi-skilling and making sure that they run on a lean and mean basis, individuals too should take advantage of the situation to upgrade themselves so that they are ready for the new changes and challenges that are going on in the various organizations and in the business community.

Provider F sees the importance of the factor as very crucial because their members are professional accountants. The respondent sees a need for their members to constantly update themselves in terms of their experiences. They need to advise their clients on the latest financial status, laws pertaining to finance and investment, taxation and advice on the budget speech made by the Finance Minister of Malaysia.

The institution also encourages members to fulfill CPE requirements. As Provider F asserts that:

> "...in fact at the association we do encourage our members to fulfill CPE requirements and recently in a discussion with the council, we may make CPE compulsory for our members to obtain Fellowship status and to be eligible, the individual has to clock in 35 CPE hours per year for three consecutive years

Provider G sees this factor as very essential to their organization. Being a public university, Provider G is conscious of their name in the market and the program they provide. Provider G explains that this factor is important because the staffs and employees need to update themselves in accordance to what is needed in the employers' market. The organization sees dynamic changes in the workplace and in the business sector. They also note that the organization needs to update their employees according to the changing scenarios. Theories and concepts are important to the students but they need to be taught on the 'how to'. Provider G also sees the relevance of this factor towards the individual. Individuals need to update themselves in accordance to the changing business conditions so that they can match into a job. They need to see what is needed in the job market and update themselves accordingly.

Provider H finds this factor paramount to both the organization and the individual. Many organizations are seen updating their employees to compete in the competitive environment, and according to Provider H:

> "...but many employers are not too clear on how to upgrade and update their employees and what areas are needed to look into. Sometimes they send their employees for updating without knowing what precisely they want the employee to learn. Their ability to analyze the need of their own business is limited"

On the other hand, the importance of this factor to the individual is significant, because the individual needs to be a valuable asset for him/her to be employed. The individual needs to be more flexible at the workplace, with the changing times to be a multitasked worker.

Provider H also emphasizes that this factor is equally important to the individual. Individuals should not wait for the employers to send them for updates. The onus is on themselves to keep abreast on current issues and updating on new skills and knowledge needed. Provider H asserts that:

> "…the knowledge base worker needs to update himself in this fast changing environment. People become out-of-date by the time they graduate from any form of program, which means that the only way to survive either at an individual level or organizational one; or even to some extent the whole country, is to keep on learning. We have a lot of learning done but transfer of that learning to workplace does not take place"

Provider I find this factor significant to both the individual and the organization. The need to update oneself seems to be a personal challenge to the individual. They also believe in life-long learning, which occurs anytime, anywhere, and across any life style. The institution also believes in training their employees for about 150 hours, over a month, every year, and this program is decentralized all over the country. Provider also finds that staff meeting can be a learning ground. They consider conducting meetings to be developmental. Provider I explains, "…I also believe when we talk about learning, for me, meetings are not just routine meetings, they are developmental whereby we learn through process learning, using mindfulness."

According to literature search, this factor seems to be important to all the institutions. The stakeholders' call to develop all those involved in the various businesses as well as public and private institutions are the rapid changes, which is taking place in the business, the workplace and the knowledge world.

In a paper presented at a conference at the University of Alberta, Cervero (1998) cites that with rapid social changes, explosion of research-based knowledge and technological innovations, leaders saw the need to continually prepare people for 40 years of professional practice through continuing education.

He goes on to explain that:

"...we began to see embryonic evidence of systems of continuing education. For example; several professions proposed plans for systems of lifelong professional education; all professions now use continuing education as a basis for re-licensure. All professions have systems of accreditation for continuing education providers and billions of dollars are spent on providing and attending continuing education programs. Furthermore, nearly every university sponsors CPE programs either through its various professional schools such as medicine, social work and engineering, in particular, certificate programs that issue documents of completion and at times, an accreditation to students"

Professional Associations the world over is the major provider of continuing education. In fact, education is one of the major, if not the primary function of associations. Furthermore, in order to keep up with change, individuals and organizations must be able to develop new skills and knowledge. CPE is playing a crucial role in the lives of professionals as they adapt to the volatile business environment. Professionals, organizations and providers must have the ability to respond quickly to changing market conditions, to government policies and the business sector as a whole.

The importance of CPE is central to professional and organizational success. Clyne (1995) summaries aptly the importance of CPE to the individual as keeping abreast in the dynamic business market, updating themselves in new knowledge, training themselves for additional roles demanded of them and improving personal effectiveness. The professional bodies play a role of policing; safeguard standards so that the public has confidence in the maintaining of competence. Professional bodies also create CPE curricula and attempt to monitor compliance.

The institution plays an important role in CPE by providing professional service to their clients. Ideally, CPE should be a joint responsibility between the individual's competence and organization's work requirement. Finally, the importance of CPE to the provider is to understand the needs of the subsequent three 'clients' as they need to learn what is required in the market place and provide that need to the respective clients so as to prepare them for the next business challenge.

Ownership of CPE

The second contextual factor is ownership of CPE. Who actually owns CPE? Is it the organization, the individual or the provider? Research shows that the ownership of CPE lies squarely on all three parties. This factor is associated with CPE practices through the question of ownership. Each party has a contribution to make towards the success of the CPE programs being conducted. All parties should give support because the end result is almost always positive. Having said this, there are some parties who argue that the ownership of CPE lies with the institution, the provider or the individual. This is in relation to the accountability of who pushes and recognizes CPE.

In this context, Provider A feels that all three parties should own CPE. The employing agency should push for the competency standards needed to achieve results and the provider should provide the training that is based on needs to support the organization to achieve results. The individual then needs to develop the skills and competency according to the standard required by the employing agency to undertake the work requirements. If all three parties work in tandem, only then would they achieve their goals equally. Thus, it is advisable for the parties concerned to set certain standards and goals so that each party can claim ownership of CPE. Providers see the ownership of CPE by all three parties. Provider B asserts:

> "...the institution must run CPE programs to say that there are people who are interested in updating themselves and this leads to a learning organization. The individual must own it because he decides what he wants to do. The employee himself must set their life goals, a life long learning contract and for the provider - if she is a training provider - must see what are the needs of the individual and therefore update them accordingly"

They further emphasized that training should be quality oriented and not quantity oriented. Provider C finds that the ownership of CPE is with the individual. This factor influences the individual in requesting the needs or related programs to be conducted for the development of the individual. As such this need enhances the individual both personally and professionally. The role played by the provider is as an updater of the latest programs and the latest topics and consecutively, they leave it to the individuals to attend. The organization plays the role of supporting both the parties.

Provider C explains that:

> "…I would like to think that as the organization, it is our role to ensure that our members are constantly updated but as a provider that makes us a training division. Here we have to source for speakers, topics and to find relevant issues that are current and informative for our members. At the same time, they do recommend certain topics where we source competent speakers for the individuals

Provider C also notices that the individuals' return on investment seems to be good. The individuals or members are very well updated and are more knowledgeable, and as such could advise their board of directors or clients competently. This is also seen from the positive feedback received from all three parties, namely the organization, the provider and the individual. Provider C expounds that it is very rare that they have a program where members say that they found the entire session to be a waste of time. Therefore, Provider C sees that the ownership of CPE is with the individual with good support from both the organization and the provider. This factor indirectly shapes CPE practices for the individual and the provider.

Provider D leaves the ownership of CPE to the market forces and the industry because in the case of Provider D, market forces shape CPE for the individuals. In that sense, the market forces will drive the parties concerned to organize and update on the latest topics and issues needed by the industry. Furthermore, CPE is mandatory and it is a legislative requirement by the Board to impose 10 CPE units per year before members of Provider D can renew their certificate of practice. In the case of Provider D, the parties who are involved in the ownership of CPE are the Board of Valuers, Appraisers and Estate Agents, Provider D, the providers and the individuals. The Board regulates the industry whereas Provider D organizes the programs for the individuals. Provider D sometimes conducts CPE training programs as well.

Provider D articulates that CPE programs should be market driven. If it's market driven it fulfills a need. There are many requirements by the members; therefore there are many CPE programs. They further add that it will come to a stage whereby people attend CPE programs because the topics are good and not because it's mandatory. From exponential research and market outlook over the year, all the parties have always owned CPE. More so by the individual because the individual is expected to be knowledgeable in the relevant issues such as laws relating to property, property taxation and sound investment in properties. The clients are placing their lifetime investments in the hands of the individuals, who, therefore need to be well versed with the latest updates to serve the real estate industry.

Provider E notices that this factor is associated with individuals. Individuals should own it and they should push organizations to sponsor them. The provider runs the topics based on the need of the organization and the individual. In the case of Provider E, CPE policies are in a developmental stage and manpower and budget is needed to run this department independently. Provider E expresses that the individual should own CPE and that if there is a budget allocation by the organization for updates, then the individual should speak to the relevant person concerned to ensure that the opportunity for development is provided.

Provider E further expounds that the individual should identify the concerned needs, whether knowledge, skill or expertise and request the organization to sponsor for the updates. Provider E further expresses:

> "…when the individual returns from the update, the knowledge and skills learnt will be transferred to the organization thus sharing the knowledge learnt. At the same time, the provider being an expert in the relevant field has updated and shared his expertise with the individual so that the individual can

put it to practice into the organization. If you really have the knowledge in you, you can't keep it but share it"

Provider F has no policy on CPE but encourages the individuals who are also self- directed learners to attend CPE programs. These three parties as being associated with CPE practices see this factor of ownership. The professional body sees the importance of professional development and the individuals are also seen as keen updaters. The institution also emphasizes the updating of their employees because it enhances their knowledge in their businesses professionally. The clients are happy and keep returning to them for advice or for more business transactions. At the same time, individuals need to update themselves to upgrade their membership professionally. Provider F asserts that:

> "…our organization will definitely continue to encourage our members to attend CPE's because we do see the importance of such professional development courses but the thing is, without the realization from the individual there is nothing much we can do. The urge to update and upgrade themselves must come from them. Only then will they attend. Else, they will have one thousand and one excuses."

Provider G remarked that the ownership of the CPE should be with the three parties. The organization should encourage employees to attend the various updates and the provider should see to it that the needs of the organization and the individual are looked into in preparing the curriculum. The individual needs to own it as he/she would be in the best position to know what he/she is lacking in and thus by updating the required knowledge, skill and attitude, the individual should be able to contribute towards organization goals.

Respondent H supports that the ownership of CPE should be the responsibility of all three parties: the organization, the individual and the provider. The institution should provide the resources, finance, libraries and set policies and monitor the outcomes of the CPE. The individual should have the ownership to choose which CPE programs to attend and to update. The providers should conduct programs depending on a need basis. This tryst agreement would enhance all parties' concerned to reach their goals and objectives towards their stakeholders. Provider H affirms that:

"...all three organizations need to own CPE. The organization will provide the resources, set the policy and monitor to make sure that people are in fact doing what they have to do. The individual will still, I think in the academic environment, have the ownership on them to choose the learning event which they think are relevant to their needs all the time. The Dean of our faculty can provide advice and guidance to the various unit heads on what they need to improve

As such, all parties have a say in the CPE practices being undertaken and which could help in the achievement of their goals.

Provider I feels that CPE ownership should be negotiated between all concerned parties. The organization may see things from a generic point of view, the department may see it from a specialist point of view and the individual may have personal interest. Therefore, matching of interest plays a very important role between the individual and the company. As Provider I points out, CPE should be negotiated, because it should be priority. There are basically generic skills; specialized skills and personal interest and if you do not allow the individual to have a personal interest it may not match. So there must be a matching of the individual's interest and that of the institution's.

From the above case analysis, it is evident that contextual factors are associated with CPE practices in one or any one of the parties: the individual, the organization or the provider. Most professional organizations see that all three parties own CPE whereas, Provider C and E think that the individual should own it. In this context the ownership of CPE can be categorized into three levels, namely the individual, the organization and the provider.

There is always a dilemma on who owns CPE learning. From a purely logical standpoint, the organization has its business objectives to consider and it has to provide a knowledge management structure so that learning at work is shared and is of benefit to the organization as a whole. CPE learning has to be relevant to the evolving strategy. At the same time, the individual needs to identify what learning the individual requires to be competent at the workplace and whether it is in line with the individual's goal of development.

Ram (1998) saw the responsibility for CPE as resting with the individual and their own personal drive for achievement. He asserts that, *"...the focus of CPE is persons and not institutions or organizations. It is not blind. It has an intellectual dimension carrying with it insight, recognition, awakening, personal knowledge and deep understanding."*Bromfield (1998) agrees to what Ram says and emphasizes that, *"...in my professional experience as a laboratory superintendent and as a training officer, I have found that WIIFM's keep people going (What's In It For Me.)."* As a provider of CPE, most of the institutions think that the ownership of CPE is with them.

The opinion of literature is that the provider only plans and provides curriculum development for the individual and the organization. In this context, it is seen that the professional association plays a dual role as a provider of updates and keeping a membership register for her members. Houle (1983) describes a provider of CPE as:

> "...at a minimum, CPE appears to be a complex of instructional systems, many of them heavily didactic, in which people who know something teach it to those who do not know it. The central aim of such teaching, which is offered by many providers, is to keep professionals up-to-date in their practice."

Providers like universities have a number of strengths as CPE organizers. They have facilities for research and development and ample resources to conduct CPE programs at any level, and they have large financial allocation compared to other smaller providers of CPE.

Professional associations too provide a range of updates and organize conferences. Houle (1990) shares that associations have direct access to professionals who are seeking continuing education and familiar with their learning needs. In this context Provider I concludes with the possibility of the factor of ownership being associated with CPE practices which are being negotiated and, responsibilities being shared between the individual, the organization and the provider.

Planning CPE Programs and Updates

The third contextual factor associated with CPE practices are planning CPE programs and updates organized by the providers. Provider A does not have a planning framework to conduct CPE programs and updates. They provide updates in an unstructured manner to their members in the form of informal tea-talks or one to two day short developmental programs. Some of the programs include train-the trainer, managing industrial relations and human resource development.

Speakers are drawn in from external or internal sources and programs are held at the venue of the organization or in a hotel. The members of the organization usually receive a brochure, memo or a reminder with regards to the unscheduled programs. When asked what is the planning model used, the provider explains that there is none, but that they are trying to develop a model in line with the Institute of Personal and Development, UK. Currently, they just run training programs for the members and the public in general.

Provider B supports the same idea put forward by provider A because of similarities in the nature of profession. Provider B considers CPE updates as non-formal requirements for membership upgrading, but at the same time the need is there to encourage members to update themselves.

In this instance, Provider B does run programs pertaining to the needs of the members and the general public. The programs conducted by provider B are train-the-trainer, certificate / diploma programs. Some of these programs are short two-day programs and some of the programs are on a long-term basis. The institution also invites members for their monthly tea-talks and convention. As Provider B expresses, they have opportunities for members to come and listen and share ideas with other trainers. They conduct one-day programs on certain topics required by their members. They also have tea-meetings on various topics and this also aids in networking. The topics shared by the resource person provide some new knowledge, skills and ideas to work on for those attending CPE programs. These updates do help the individual and the organization.

Provider C does not have a structure or a model on planning CPE programs but they do run CPE programs. It is a one or a two-day program and it can also be in the form of a convention or forum. These are updates to provide the latest scenario in the business sector. The agency needs to update their members with the latest changes of the legislations, regulations and corporate governance as a director of a company. These updates are crucial for the members because their clients depend on them to provide sound business advice.

As Provider C explains, their members need to be continually updated. They have to be advised on any legislature changes, regulation changes and the only way a lot of members can get these changes is through them, the professional body. Some of the CPE programs conducted by the organization include company secretarial duties, ethics and corporate governance, how-to topics such as applying for required licenses and soft skills programs.

Provider D conducts CPE programs because it is mandatory and according to the legislation governing the practice of the industry. Provider D conducts CPE programs consisting of technical to soft skills. They also organize tea-talks, luncheons talks and conventions. They encourage members to attend the programs to clock 10 CPE units before they are allowed to renew their certificate of practice. Members are also encouraged to attend international conferences in various countries to gain different perspectives of the CPE practices of the profession. Most of the CPE programs are tailored to the need of the individual.

Like any other professional organization, Provider D conducts half-day to two-day CPE programs relevant to the industry. This includes programs for their members as well as their employees. Some of the programs organized are real estate negotiators courses, property law, sale and purchase agreements, understanding strata titles and others to name a few. Provider D asserts that he programs or updates are for the principals and their employees. The programs would cover everything from technical aspects to marketing, human relationship to negotiation to statute changes. These programs provide value to the members. They go back enriched with new updates from the input provided by the various speakers. Provider D goes on to share that they look at it from the fact that when they have an education seminar, it is for their benefit. They take home value from anyone of these seminars that they attend.

Provider E conducts CPE updates to develop their employees and their members. Program planning of CPE is still new, and records of CPE points attended by members are not kept. The individuals do not keep these records, as attending CPE updates is not compulsory. Provider E does conduct relevant programs for their member's interest to update them on the latest changes in the business sector. As management accountants, clients are advised on financial matters pertaining to the business and management budget. Even though the institution finds it difficult to run these CPE programs, they know that they need to update their members who are professionals.

They conduct programs that namely consist of corporate governance, management accounting, cost control and soft skills programs. Most of these updates are conducted for one or two days. The provider also organizes conventions and invite a series of resource speakers internally and externally to contribute towards the topics. According to Provider E, the committee would decide to lay down at least twenty topics. Twenty relevant topics and they may find this more useful, more beneficial to their members. By conducting these CPE programs and updates, the organization is actually updating their members professionally to keep abreast of changing times. There, however, is a lack of program development framework with Provider E.

Provider F has a compulsory system for their members to clock in 35 CPE units per year. This is a requirement for their members to upgrade themselves to the next level. As such, Provider F runs at least seventy CPE program updates on relevant topics for her members. This includes one or two day programs, conventions, forums and tea-talks. The speakers are from the institutions or are invited from other professional bodies.

The institution sees the update for their members as a wholesome development. They conduct technical as well as soft skill developmental programs According to Provider F who expounds the need to be well versed not only in auditing, but also financial management, taxation and accounting. They also provide updates to expose themselves to generic issues that include soft skills and consider this as part of professional development. This is especially so for those who want to move away from technical matters to management and realize the importance of the soft skills to get them there.

Some of the topics they organize include communication, presentation skills and teambuilding to name a few. These programs usually garner good response. CPE program updates are run professionally with brochures sent out to all members. In turn, the provider receives at least 20 to 30 participants who attend the workshop to update themselves and are very happy to have received such updates. Provider F consists of a program planning committee who looks at the development of new programs and updates.

Provider G plays the role of a public provider of CPE program updates. These CPE program updates are short-term programs lasting from 24 to 52 weeks; after which these short-term programs may lead the individuals to degree programs. The provider provides to the need of the general public who may want to update themselves. The provider plays the role of an extension school by designing programs for adults. Some of the programs offered are certificate and diploma in childhood development, human resource development, accounting and finance, forensic science and study tours to name a few.

The provider also conducts in-house programs especially to the public listed companies, government sectors and the uniform agencies. The provider also trains and updates participants from overseas who comes in on an attachment for about 6-9 months to study our working system. According to then, they need to manage the updates, as it is part of the university's policy. The market wants to progress with new updates and they investigate and study the market conditions on what is needed in the changing business sector, and that is what they provide to the adult learner. Planning CPE programs and updates are reviewed by a full time training and education committee.

Provider H may not have a CPE policy, but the agency has a philosophy that academic staff is required to constantly learn pertaining to their field of study and profession. The individuals are recommended to attend programs every year to update themselves. The Institution allocates large amounts of money for providing updates to their members. Some of these updates are very expensive because of the specialized field they maybe attached to. The faculty head and her committee comprising of full time employees organize CPE program planning and updates.

Provider H remarks that some of these CPE program updates are very expensive. Some of these events are held overseas, like conferences, or short-term workshops relating to the field of study. In such institutions, the onus of CPE program updates is on the individual. The allocation of budget is there, but the individual has to source out the event and apply for it. The only CPE update provided by the agency to the individual is the induction course, which last for about 6 to 12 months.

Some individuals update themselves by reading the latest journals and surf the Internet for the latest issues. On the other hand, the institution also identifies those who do not have the time to attend updates, and provide them with support by sharing their research with their colleagues whereby feedback is provided. Some of these programs are conducted internally for the staff and at other times, outsiders are invited to be trainers in adult education, retail management, how to use training aids and soft skill programs.

Provider I encourages the individuals to attend updates or programs that are relevant to their field. Individuals are recommended to attend 150 hours of CPE in a year. After attending, participants are required to share the experience or what they have learnt at the workplace. Provider I also insists that all lecturers and staff must conduct research, write papers and co-present papers at conferences and conventions both nationally and internationally.

The respondent also creates opportunities for the staff members and lecturers to present papers with him. This provides confidence to the employees on the 'how to' and they would have learnt from an expert of more than 40 years. Furthermore, the provider explains that after attending programs or updates, the participants are required to send a copy of a set of notes to the library and also to distribute the relevant materials to all concerned for reading purposes.

Sometimes, the writing of reviews and presentation on the subject matter by the attendees to colleagues is also required. This provides a good learning experience for the individual and for the organization; it has fulfilled the part of updating the individual with the necessary knowledge, skills and competencies required by the individual to face the various stakeholders.

In conducting, interpreting and analyzing the literature available, most of the institutions plan, organize and conduct CPE programs and updates. The question on the mind of everyone is, is there a CPE model or a mixture of models being practiced? On the other hand, CPE for professions as a field of educational practice is still at an infant stage and underdeveloped in Malaysia. Many of the concepts, theories, and practice procedures are from the models of professional education from the universities.

Most groups involved in CPE practices such as professional associations, employers and providers may have knowledge of professional practice and work settings but they may lack understanding of educational and research processes. Nowlen (1988) describes three curriculum development models of CPE that are beneficial models from a range of perspectives. These models have been discussed in chapter three, under the literature review. In this case, all or most of the respondents conduct CPE programs using the update model, in accordance to the needs of the individual and the organization.

This promotes the effective practice of CPE whereby concepts and the resource person shares theories. According to Schon (1983), professionals often say that when they are applying a research-based technique or protocol, that is when their problem solving is firmly grounded in the world of certainty, stability and rigor. The 'Update Model' seems to be the model practiced by most of the providers. Some of the programs organized by providers that are considered as updates are presentation skills, finance for non-finance executives and laws relating to property to name a few.

Houle (1982), sums-up the 'update model' as:

> "...at minimum, continuing professional education appears to
> be a complex of instructional systems, many of them heavily
> didatic, in which people who know something teach it to those
> who do not know it. The central aim of such teaching, which
> is offered by many providers, is to keep professionals up to date
> in their practice. But the achievement of this goal is usually

evaluated indirectly, chiefly by counting the number of people involved in an activity or assessing their attitude toward it."

This captures the model explained which provides for the organizing of the various programs which includes methodologies used, case studies, simulations and interactive games. Even though these methods add live to the programs, it is often dominated by informational updates, running two to three days. Thus, these 'knowledge updates' or 'technology transfers' are considered as updating the professionals with the latest information in management or technologies.

One may ask, how is this related to enhancing competency, proficiency and performance? This is anybody's guess, as this is the practice of professional associations and providers of CPE. Incidentally, the strength of this update model lies in the following; the update model provides practicing professionals with a level of knowledge comparable to professionals graduating from professional schools. It closes the gap created by the rapid changes in technology, science and skills between the old and young professionals (Nowlen,1988).The introduction of this model has affected well the curriculum of the professional schools and being up-to-date is one important aspect of the relationship between knowledge and skill.

One must remember that being up-to-date does not guarantee a higher level of competency and performance by professionals. Validity of curriculum developed in the update model does not measure the new competency of professionals after three days of participation. Learning new competency or measurement of competency is any part of curriculum development in the update model.

The data analysis also shows respondents D, F, H and I plan CPE programs using the 'competence model'. This model is generally defined as marked or sufficient aptitude, skill, strength, judgment or knowledge without noticeable weakness or demerit. To be competent is to possess sufficient knowledge and ability to meet specified requirements in the sense of being able, adequate, suitable and capable. Baehr (1984) said competence is a measure of both capacity to perform and performance itself.

The members being in these respective organizations need to be competent to serve their clients. In this context, employers, professional associations, higher educational institutions have taken serious steps in developing standards, evaluation, certification and recertification, licensure and planning for organizing and conducting long term CPE programs and updates.

Collaborative Relationship

The fourth contextual factor associated with CPE practices is collaborative relationships. Most, if not all agencies collaborate with other providers to offer CPE programs. This pooling of resources is to avoid duplication of resources be it financially or inviting resource speakers. Some agencies develop collaborative relationship with providers from overseas to offer long term programs which lasts for 12 to 15 months. Some are short-term programs, lasting for 4 to 6 weeks. Providers sometimes organize joint venture CPE programs to enhance the program as well as to have bigger participation by exhibitors and attendees in the programs to avoid financial loss.

Provider A organizes a number of programs, which is in collaboration with other similar agencies. They also organize joint workshops, conventions and support independent providers by lending their name. Provider A explains that it is a necessity to collaborate with similar providers so that they can pool the resources, be it finance, speakers or venues and moreover the participants hold dual membership in similar agencies. Some of the agencies that collaborate with Provider A are governmental agencies, the uniform staff and the private agencies providing CPE programs.

Provider B collaborates with other similar training and development bodies. Of late there are a number of request by other providers who want to collaborate with provider B. Provider B is in collaboration with the University of Malaya center for extension education and Sunway College. Some of the CPE programs offered are certificate in training and development and the trainer series programs.

According to Provider B, they have programs in collaboration with the government agencies, and multi-national companies, but they would need to be selective in who they are collaborating with. Their image as an institution may be at stake should they collaborate with the wrong agency or organization. Provider B also collaborates with the telecommunication companies providing CPE programs in training and development.

Provider C has a free hand to collaborate with agencies who have similar programs or otherwise. Provider C collaborates with independent providers as well as government agencies like the Commercial Commission of Malaysia to conduct CPE programs related to company directors. Provider C states that their collaborative relationships are with University Utara Malaysia and University Malaya where programs are related to corporate governance and company secretarialship. These programs are either conducted as short or long term programs for both their members and the general public. The respondent also emphasizes that short programs of one to two days are also organized in cooperation with private providers. Conventions are sponsored by relevant agencies that have an interest in the agency and members of the institution.

Provider D believes in collaboration relationships with other CPE providers. At present, Provider D collaborates with the Board of Valuers, appraisers and estate agents who organize compulsory CPE programs. The board conducts the Diploma in estate management with Provider D being the institution that manages estate agents in Malaysia. At the same time, Provider D enhances the image of her members by developing a collaborative relationship with the National Realtors Association in USA. By inviting their members to speak at the conventions or workshops organized by the institution, the participation at the conference increases and the institution makes a profit. Provider D chooses whom they want to collaborate with carefully because of the issues of conflict of interest. Provider D sharedthat2 years ago,they collaborated with the National Association of Realtors, USA to organize a conference over two days, and they were the first to do it. It was very successful whereby; they had 250 members and guests attending. They had the president of the National Association of Realtors and some top speakers coming from the USA to speak at the conference. They also have a bilateral working relationship with other real estate associations in the world

The local banks and the newspaper agencies usually cosponsor programs organized by Provider D because members of the agency do refer their clients to the banks for financial matters. Other collaborative relationships are with the Developers Association of Malaysia and the Institute of Surveyors Malaysia.

Provider E has collaborations with other agencies, one of them being the Employers Federation of Malaysia. Provider E ventures with private agencies to provide job opportunities for their student membership. The institution too, invites speakers from the parent company in UK to facilitate at workshops or seminars. Currently, Provider E is aggressively looking for collaborative partners to help market their CPE program and updates.

Provider F plays a positive role in collaborative partnership. They collaborate with the Malaysian Institute of Investment Analysis, the Malaysian Institute of Accountants and other professional bodies. They also have the full support on collaboration from their parent company in the UK. To develop public speaking and build confidence in their members, Provider F has collaborated with Toastmaster International to set up a speaking club for their members. Jointly, Provider F organizes conferences with universities and independent providers. One of their main collaborative partnership that was a success is with a government agency who overseas the small and medium size industry.

According to the Provider, they have a link-up with a few government organizations including SMIDEC and MIDA where joined efforts are made to organize seminar/workshops updates on how to raise funds, business loans and advise on business investments. The institution also collaborates with employment agencies to help their student members to find job placements.

In the case of Provider G, collaborative cooperation is with other government agencies, the uniformed agencies and the private university colleges. As much as provider G runs programs for the adults, they still franchise their 'branded' programs around the country. Some of the programs include certificate in childhood development, human resource development and secretarial management. Provider G states that collaborative partnerships with university/college INTI in accountancy and APPIT on information technology are in progress. Provider G also has a bilateral arrangements to train employees of local and foreign government agencies on various issues relating to education, economics, youth development, forensic science and corporate governance, to name a few.

Provider H asserts that it's very rare or unwritten reason in having a collaboration relationship with outside agencies. During the 1990s and before the financial crisis, Provider H had collaborative arrangements with universities from the USA. Since then, these collaborative efforts have been reduced because of high costs of sending scholars over to their country.

Currently, there are attempts to collaborate with local and private providers of CPE programs. The collaborative partnership are based on programs like interior design, retail management and hotel catering whereby joint ventures are made with the local retail chains, hotels and the private sector. There are also signs of hosting international conferences in collaboration with CPE providers.

Provider I has a special comment on collaborative relationships. According to them, there are 70,000 non-governmental organizations and not all of these are professional organization. At the same time, not all professional organizations are managed professionally, because of the part time effort. So the ideals are there to collaborate but depending on the various bodies and the interest that they have. The institution goes on to say that there must be synergy, a win-win situation especially when the agency is privately run and has to show a profit to the Board of Directors.

The research shows that most, if not all the institutions have some sought of collaborative arrangement with each other. A central finding of the body of research shows that any understanding of collaboration of continuing education has to recognize the larger organizational goals being pursued through the formation of such relationships. It is also noted that by having collaborative relationships with professional bodies, private providers, and universities there are possibilities for the various providers to increase their student intake as well as membership.

In a research by Cervero (1984), it was found that a primary reason medicals schools have extensive collaborative relationships with community hospitals is to increase the number of patient referrals to the university hospital. On this same note, Providers A, B, C, D, E and F collaborates with private providers and sponsors to reduce the cost of conducting CPE programs, be it seminars, workshops or conventions. By sponsoring the programs, the sponsors also get mileage by advertising within the booklets or banners, and members do enquire the products marketed by the sponsors. Thus, a win-win situation as suggested by Provider I.

These relationships among providers have been described by such terms as cooperation (Beder, 1984), collaboration (Cervero 1984), partnership (Nowlen and Stern, 1981), and interdependence (Fingeret 1984). Cervero and Young (1987) had proposed six qualitatively different strategies. They are monopoly, parallelism, competition, cooperation, coordination and collaboration. This typology is intended to include any one provider relating to another provider.

Most of the providers practice the strategies of competition, cooperation and collaboration. Providers A, B, C, D, E, and F cite competition as an action strategy for CPE programs (Beders 1984 and Cross, 1981). In this orientation, two or more providers offer programs on a specific topic with full knowledge that others are doing the same. According to Azzaretto (1987), this strategy often occurs in management development programs, in which independent consultants, employer training departments, professional associations, university business departments and continuing education units all offer similar courses.

In this scenario, if there are enough participants to be shared there will be happiness. On the other hand, if there are not enough participants to go around, providers may lose money or cancel programs and thus, conflict may occur among the providers. As for cooperation, which refers to the strategy in which providers assist one another on an ad-hoc basis (Whetten, 1981). In this example, Providers D, F and G seem to practice this action strategy. They may provide the membership list to the independent providers whereby they market their programs to the members' institution and for each member enrolled, the provider may provide a rebate to the marketers. In doing so, the three providers become interdependent on a short-term basis. The last action strategy, collaboration, refers to providers 'working together jointly and continuously on a particular project towards a specific goal' (Lindsay, Queeney, and Smutz, 1981).

Providers G, H and I practice a high strategy of collaboration among the providers. They have a tendency to collaborate with the government departments, private providers, professional associations and private university/ colleges locally and internationally. They may run CPE programs such as conventions or forums and this collaboration is based on sharing of profit or by just lending the 'brand' name and is mutually agreeable most of the times.

By collaborating, the providers are sharing resources and saving costs, program planning is done with the relevant providers in mind and mutual organizational goals are met. Cervero and Collins (1998), assert that collaboration is a strategy that has been used extensively and will continue to be used to develop systems of continuing education. However, astute leaders recognize that the formation of collaborative relationships is fundamentally a political process in which costs and benefits must be clearly weighed, including those involving organizational agendas other than those connected to the continuing education program.

Thus effective partnerships will develop not from a belief that collaboration is the right thing to do, but from a definitive understanding of the goals to be achieved by the partnership, a clear recognition of the benefits to be gained by each institution, and the contribution of equivalent resources by each partner.

How The Practices Influence the Development of CPE in Malaysia

CPE practices influence the development of CPE in all nine providers but were not professionally undertaken. In this context, the providers are compared to professional providers such s The Institute of Personal and Development, UK and The American Society of Training and Development. The providers showed intentions to practice CPE but they have limitations in bringing together and understanding the role and need of the stakeholders; namely the individual, the organization and the provider.

This book also helps shed some light on the CPE practices among the providers. These practices help influence the development of CPE in the organization of the various professional providers under scrutiny. These themes emerged from the data analysis and can be seen in Table 2. They include the philosophy of CPE, professional functions, program planning and development, and program administration and evaluation.

CHAPTER 9

PHILOSOPHY OF CPE

As we move into the new millennium, many professional vocations are becoming increasingly aware of the mounting external pressures of global competitiveness and of the internal demands of their people for peace, prosperity and a better quality of life. Demands are made for more effective and efficient systems of education and training and development to meet the overlapping needs of the governments, the industry and commerce and of individuals. Resources are limited and the learner/employee profile is becoming more complex and the quality requirements more exacting. In an effort to insure quality, many professions now require CPE for re-certification or re-licensure. Other than the medical, legal and/or the engineers' professions, the accounting, audit and real estate professions too now require CPE to continue their practice.

The evidence obtained from the research shows that most of the professional associations and providers do not have a policy or regulate CPE and managed rudimentary. The management of CPE is generally an issue yet to be recognized as an activity worthy of management time. There was frequently an absence of coherent CPE policy that reflects business-driven needs. CPE is perceived as just a special type of developmental activity. Thus there is little attempt to relate professional development activities to strategic business objectives.

At the same time, challenges faced by the continuing educators or providers of CPE have been manifold and the pace of change is accelerating in recent years. From the research, the providers have shared their opinions and views concerning the challenges faced by them. Provider B sees the challenge of professionalism as a major concern. According to them, not many members understand the word 'professional' and they have an uncharacteristic attitude towards this. They are the 'know all' and thus, challenge the agency in non-attendance of CPE programs.

Professions are simply those occupations that have gained professional status. Cervero (1988) identifies the following six characteristics as essential for an occupation to claim professional status. Professions must (1) involve in intellectual operations, (2) derive their material from science, (3) involve definite and practical ends, (4) possess an educationally communicable technique, (5) tend to self-organization, and (6) be altruistic.

Provider B agrees to the above definition but expounds that enforcement is a problem because there is a lack of resources, be it finance or manpower to handle the issue of attendance by members. Therefore, the members take an upper hand to manipulate issues according to how they can manage it. Furthermore, the committee or the council members are made up of the same people. According to Provider A, who agrees to what Provider B claims, explains that as long as there is no legislation or mandatory rule to practice the profession, members will not take CPE seriously.

The challenge faced by Provider I is leadership. Provider I questions the leader of the organization and how the leader can help the organization in terms of introducing CPE. They see this as a challenge because an organization must have a visionary leader and must support the growth of the individual. Only when the individual grows in knowledge, can the organization grow. The leader should also tie CPE with the business strategy of the organization so that new skills are learnt and applied to enhance bottom line Cervero, and Schon (1988, p. 158) suggested that:

> "... as a leader, this process can be coached and not taught. Faculty in graduate programs and workshop presenters, for example, can assume the role of coaches by explaining how they would perform in given practice situations and by reflecting with participants on the ways in which they approach similar situations."

Professional Function

Discussion concerning CPE has tended to focus on either the needs of the individual professionals or the interests of the professional bodies. There are other stakeholders who could have a legitimate interest in the effective management of CPE. These include organizations employing professional staff, non-professional employees, the government, CPE providers and the clients of professional practitioners. This CPE practice of professional function discusses the evidence gained from data analysis, pertaining to the ways in which organizations seek to manage CPE of employees whom they support through developmental activities. Professionals belong to professional bodies that seek to encourage or require members to demonstrate evidence of CPE for re-certification or practice. The expectation is that learning and development will become planned and organized. It is also noted that there is a conflict about the ownership of CPE. The fact that all three parties, being the individual, the institution and the provider own CPE are confirmed by providers D, E, and F. A similar research conducted in the United Kingdom on providers concurs with the respondents (Jones and Robinson, 1998). They go on to say that individual development needs accord with business imperatives, and a shared responsibility between the individual and the organization.

Provider D argues that the ownership is market driven, and according to them the ownership is market driven. If programs are good, the members will attend and the provider must provide programs that are needed in the marketplace. Provider B argues that all three parties own CPE; the individual decides what program he wants to attend according to his needs and the provider/organization conducts the program according to the need of the stakeholders. The above arguments are in line with Clyne (1995, p. 19) who asserts that for the individual there are three common reasons for professionals to engage in CPE. These are to update themselves in new knowledge, train themselves for additional roles demanded of them and improve personal effectiveness. For the individual, the initial qualification gives them a start. CPE gives them the power to choose and change direction according to market development. As for the professional bodies, they play roles of a professional educator and CPE provider. Among others, they play a role by safeguarding standards so that the public has confidence in the maintenance of competence and monitoring compliance. The employer has a responsibility to their clients to provide competent and efficient professional service.

The recording of CPE activities undertaken by employees might reflect the interest of several stakeholders. Many professional bodies for example, Providers C, D, E, and F demand or encourage their members to record or log details of their professional development activities for the purpose of upgrade, re-licensure, and re-certification. The employing agency too, has an interest in monitoring CPE through the maintenance of suitable recording systems, if only to track cost implications for resource allocation purposes. Additionally, the individual professional may have an interest in maintaining accurate records of CPE work, as this may be good evidence of self-managed professional responsibilities. The practice of recording CPE information varies between the professional bodies. One of the most common formats involves a record of attendance at CPE programs. In this context, provider D, E, and F provide certificate of CPE for participants attending CPE programs. Thus, by attending these updates the professional practitioner enhances personal outcomes and performance at the workplace. The employer needs to integrate the job related competence required with what the professional body expects. The professional bodies, Providers D, E, F, G and H however, make it very clear in their literature that CPE is a partnership between the employee, employer, provider and the professional body. Furthermore, this practice of CPE should be rooted in and viewed as an extension of professional education.

Competence evolves over time, and effective learning is a long term, cumulative and integrated process (Cervero,1990).This practice and factor should be viewed as part of the lifelong learning continuum and development of a mindset toward how continuing education should begin prior to practice. This practice should also be looking into the professional as an adult learner. Program design and delivery should emphasize consultation and cooperation, and not coercion. Professionals can be given broad parameters in their selection and design of their individual learning programs. Cervero (1990), gave the following description of professionals as learners: professionals construct an understanding of current situations of practice using a repertoire of practical knowledge acquired primarily through experience in prior 'real life' situations. CPE practices must foster practical knowledge and know-how as well as critical reflection.

Program Planning and Development

CPE providers should understand that they should take heed of what the members 'needs' are before coming out with programs. Awareness of these aims is necessary components of effective practice. Being an effective CPE provider requires a clear and explicit recognition of the place of the professions in society. Without this understanding, educators are left without an important tool for making decisions in their daily practice and ultimately for improving their practice. Cervero (1988, p.18) sums up aptly, *"what it is, why it is, and what it should be in proper perspective, thereby giving sound and purposeful direction to practice...[and] it can provide the necessary framework for examining our key assumptions regarding learners, providers, and the content and process".*

The study shows that there are no systematic program planning and development strategies developed by the providers of CPE. These units are either run by employed, volunteer executives or council members who do not have the experience in program planning and development strategies. Program planners should use a stakeholder based planning model by taking into account the needs and interests of the internal and external stakeholders, or people who significantly affect or are affected by the program. When they do, the program is more likely to be implemented well, achieve its objectives, and garner enough support to be sustained. Planners must also be able to identify the relevant stakeholders groups and how they relate to and depend on one another; understand their interests in relation to the program; build a planning and implementation process that takes heed of their situation, needs and interests into account; and evaluate all the programs' processes and effects to see how the groups are being served and what can be improved (Cervero, and Wilson, 1994; Umble, Cervero, and Langone, 2001).

In this context, Provider A and B agreed that they do not have a qualified program planner in their organization. Programs are planned according to a gut feel and what other competitors offer. As much as the various providers try to plan their programs well, it still has to be approved by the council members or the faculty. Some of these programs, printed in brochure forms, do not have sufficient content and also do not have an outcome. According to Provider E, they sometimes download certain programs from the website related to the profession and then make changes accordingly. After that they print the brochures and run the program. Many of the respondents agreed to have a program planner who is an amateur but was quick to say that it is costly to employ a professional program planner. Providers C, E and F found that there are too many similar professional bodies catering for the same members. Their suggestion is to merge the various bodies or share the resources. This would save cost and manpower and provide a more efficient and effective support system. As for program planning and development strategies, a suggestion was made to collaborate among the professional bodies instead of duplicating the programs and having poor attendance and losing money in the venture.

Brookfield (1986), argues that professional providers are skeptics and usually do not want to collaborate. Personal conflicts, political factors, resources and budgetary constraints constantly alter neatly conceived plans of action. Even though planning frameworks are successful, no continuing educator shares this framework with others. They are influenced by their own personal values and beliefs and the institutional context they work in. Cervero and Schon (1988), encourage CPE educators to be reflective practitioners, if they want to be engaged in this important task. Provider I also emphasizes that the leader should have sound knowledge of what is happening in the world so that the CPE programs introduced are related to business needs that meet the current challenge.

From the research point of view, the challenge faced by public CPE providers compared to the commercial providers is that whether universities and further education establishments as well as commercial learning providers look set to reap the rewards of providing CPE, should they be able to demonstrate the flexibility necessary to meet this adult learning agenda.

Having said this, there are systematic processes that have been codified as planning frameworks to provide guidance. Sork and Busky (1986) define a program development framework as *"a set of steps, tasks or decisions which, when carried out, produce the design and outcome specifications for a systematic instructional activity."* Cervero and Apps (1988) note that there are five common tasks towards a program development framework. They are: (1) identifying learners needs, (2) defining objectives, (3) identifying learning experiences that meet these objectives, (4) organizing learning experiences into an educational plan, and (5) evaluating the outcomes of the educational efforts in accordance with the objectives.

Planners and managers of education units will also want to be skilled at substantive negotiations, which are the more detailed give-and-take discussions about the programs specific content, teaching methods, audience, or marketing strategies. Planners will want to keep learner and faculty interests at the table to ensure program quality yet also be willing to compromise to meet the legitimate needs of the institution offering the program and keep costs within reasonable range. CPE educators and providers, particularly those in public and private sectors; organizations and universities, will probably be less familiar with strategic management and business planning concepts. In addition, they may have to do more education and negotiation in their organizations to bring such ideas into practice.

Boone (1985) stressed that it is important that CPE programs are linked to the participants' specific needs and requirements. As he sees it, a collaborative approach to program planning should be adopted between the providers, adult educators and the participants. Research also shows a lack of this systematic approach being undertaken to design and develop programs by the various CPE stakeholders as they see each other as competitors. As such, whatever the providers plan in their planning framework, Houle in Cervero (1988) equips that ultimately every planner of a CPE program must remain in control of whatever process, principle, or pattern he or she finds useful.

Program Administration and Evaluation

Effective performance in an organization will reflect, among other things, the administration and evaluation of the activities undertaken. It was noticed that providers have no structured system of administration and evaluation of CPE. The evaluation process is dependent on the reaction sheet provided by the providers after the seminar updates that are collected thereafter. These are then given to the CPE committee to evaluate whether the seminars have been run well or need to be improved. Most of the providers do not have an evaluating system of CPE programs. Surprisingly, the individuals do not keep a record of their attendance of CPE. Only providers, whose members need to renew their certificate of practice do keep a record for this purpose, otherwise there is none. Some of the providers only kept attendance records of CPE activity. To this effect, there is no control mechanism that could help monitor who has attended CPE programs.

Another factor that needs administering and evaluating are CPE resources such budgets, training facilities, training equipment and faculties. The organizations do want to see quantitative gains at the workplace in line with business strategy of the organization. Sanderlands (1998, p. 74) in a similar research argues that much of the money available for CPE is regarded as luxury and to be cut in hard times if the budget needs squeezing. The challenge is to make sure that CPE is focused on real projects with a return on investment that is actually demonstrable and helps meet the bottom line of the organization.

The CPE committee feels as long as the program is successfully run without complain then the program is successful. According to Cervero (1988, p. 134), there are seven categories to evaluating a CPE program. They are program design and implementation, learner participation, learner satisfaction, learner knowledge, skills and attitudes, application of learning after the program, the impact of application of learning and program characteristics associated with outcomes. All the seven categories are interlinked and anyone category should not be inferred as a success or failure of the program. Clyne's (1995) experience shows that members are keen to see a tough stance being taken on monitoring until it affects them. The tone and style of the approach is thus all important. Generally, individuals demonstrate misconceptions rather than outright obstruction.

Members need to be reminded of the CPE message and the message needs to be updated and promoted regularly by a variety of means to the members of the professional associations and providers of CPE. According to Providers H and I, who share that the evaluative procedures in the organization are based on the students and peers providing information on the program and the CPE presenter. As far as the outcome of the participants' learning, there is only a reaction sheet to fill up and for the planning committee to consider taking action later. Cervero (1988) often repeats that evaluation is a basic function of the CPE provider unit to assess its success or failure in programming; that continuing education makes a difference in professional practice and client outcomes. When it comes to evaluating the programs, the providers or the educators do not have the resources to conduct a labor-intensive type of evaluation. In most cases, continuing educators or providers administer end of program reaction sheets to participants and obtain some useful information for planning future programs.

Providers C, E and F found that there are too many similar professional bodies catering for the same members. Their suggestion is to merge the various bodies or share the resources. This would save cost and manpower and provide a more efficient and effective support system. As for program planning and development strategies, a suggestion was made to collaborate among the professional bodies instead of duplicating the programs and have poor attendance and losing money in the venture.

Provider H argues that there is no system to facilitate CPE and to monitor and evaluate those who have used the budget, since it's on a 'first come first serve basis'. They see that those participants who wanted to improve themselves took advantage of attending CPE programs, thus the provider depletes the budget on only a few employees. The challenge to put a system in place for provider H augurs well for the organization. Cervero (1988, p.148) states that:

> "…evaluation processes must be part of the larger cycle of program development, just as program development is a form of professional practice. Evaluation problems, like program planning problems are encountered in situations that are characterized by uniqueness uncertainty, and value conflicts. Providers and continuing educators, by using examples from their work place setting can determine the evaluation problems to be solved as well as how to solve them"

In summary, the above practices influence the development of CPE in the organizational settings of the various providers. It must also be noted that practice is always conducted in a context composed of varying personalities, shifting expectations, conflicting goals and limited resources. As seen from the study, practice is rooted in particular sets of circumstances; it would be inappropriate to judge efforts against some fixed ideal of good practice. Good practice is always provided by the institutional setting in which practice takes place.

CHAPTER 10

CONCLUSIONS AND IMPLICATIONS

For professionals to continue meeting the needs of their clients, a greater understanding of the connections between the context of practice and professional learning is needed. Providers and adult educators could benefit from developing a better understanding of how knowledge becomes meaningful in practice, particularly given long standing empirical and theoretical insights (Benner, 1984; Cervero, 1988; Schon, 1987) that have yet to have much impact on CPE practice. As professionals continue to be integrated into organizations, the linkages between context and practice needs to be defined and analyzed so that learning and professional practice can continue to grow in these new settings.

This book explored the theoretical concepts laid down by Houle (1980) for continuing learning in the professions. Nowlen (1988) contributes to a new approach to continuing education for the business and the professions: the performance model; and Cervero (1988) who showed effective continuing education for professionals.

Philosophy of CPE - Importance of CPE

CPE is defined as the systematic maintenance, improvement and broadening of knowledge and the development of personal qualities necessary for the education of professional and technical duties throughout the practitioners working life (Clyne, 1995). The key features of effective CPE are continuous throughout the practitioners working life; professional/organization focused necessary for the execution of professional and technical duties and related to maintaining the quality and relevance of professional services; broad based knowledge and skills and the development of personal qualities and structure of systematic maintenance improvement and broadening.

The management of CPE is generally an issue yet to be recognized as an activity worthy of management time. There was frequently an absence of coherent CPE policy that reflects business-driven needs. CPE is perceived as just a special type of developmental activity. Thus there is little attempt to relate professional development activities to strategic business objectives. Clyne (1995) suggested that it is necessary to have a policy on CPE, partly because the professional body needs to be seen to be doing something and partly because it does provide a stick with which to beat those who are failing in their professional duty and might be a danger to the general public and the workplace.

Furthermore, a CPE policy plays a necessary part in reinforcing the credibility of a professional body if it is to sustain the dual role of trade association or provider of CPE and regulator of standards. Most providers have policies and mission statements entrenched in their official documents, but the question is on implementation. Who is going to spearhead this development? Clearly, CPE providers face challenges from stakeholders, the individual, the organization and the provider. It is up to the individual to face up to the challenge. Individuals find it difficult to cope because of pressures from their jobs and the need to remain current and employable. However, the same can be said of the institution that employs these professionals, as they seek to compete through knowledge and learning. Professional institutions and learning providers must see the competition ahead in this era of emerging new knowledge and technological change and face these challenges head on.

Professional Functions - Ownership of CPE

It is imperative of the organization to sponsor CPE initiatives, while noting that individual ownership of the issue was a major factor. The providers seek senior level support in successfully nurturing individual employees to develop themselves professionally, while seeking to align this learning with the goals of the organization.

Individuals do not keep a record of their attendance of CPE. Only providers whose members need to renew their certificate of practice do keep a record for this purpose, otherwise there is none. Some of the providers only kept attendance records of CPE activity.

According to Clyne (1995), experience shows that members are keen to see a tough stance being taken on monitoring until it affects them. The tone and style of the approach is thus all important. Generally, individuals demonstrate misconceptions rather than outright obstruction. Members need to be reminded of the CPE message and the message needs to be updated and promoted regularly by a variety of means to the members of the professional associations. Almost all the respondents do not have a system on how to calculate the return on investment after attending CPE programs. Some of the respondents have seen qualitative improvements in the individuals by way of practicing what they have learnt to the workplace, but some respondents do not see that. The providers do want to see quantitative gains at the workplace in line with the business strategy of the organization.

Sandelands (1998) in his research of the same, argues that much of the money available for CPE is regarded as luxury and to be cut in hard times if the budget needs squeezing. The challenge the is to make sure that CPE is focused on real projects with an return on investment that is actually demonstrable and helps meet the bottom line of the organization. As organizations become increasingly effective at reducing costs and improving efficiency in their operations, their attention has shifted to revenue growth.

Tapping the collective creativity and know-how of employees is emerging as one of the best ways to anticipate customer needs and grow new markets. This factor is worth exploring subsequently, as to whether such establishments complement the professional providers or whether there will be a clash as each tries to claim ownership of the process. No matter what type of agency the CPE educators and members work in, the key leadership challenge is to position continuing educating activities so that they come to be seen as actively contributing to the attainment of institutional goals (Simerly,1987).

Program Planning and Development - Planning CPE Updates

There is currently no systematic program planning for CPE updates by providers of CPE. These program planning units are run either by employed or volunteer executives who do not have the experience in program planning and development strategies.

Surprisingly, Brookfield (1986) laments that the little research that has been done suggests that virtually no continuing educators use planning frameworks, even for programs that are successful. All continuing educators operate out of their own planning framework, which is influenced by their personal values and beliefs and the institutional context in which they work. Having said this, there are systematic processes that have been codified as planning frameworks to provide guidance.

Sork and Busky (1986) define a program development framework as *"a set of steps, tasks or decisions which, when carried out, produce the design and outcome specifications for a systematic instructional activity."* Boone (1985) stressed that the importance of CPE programs being linked to the participants' specific needs and requirements are crucial. As he sees it, a collaborative approach to program planning should be adopted between the providers' adult educators and the participants. There is also a lack of this systematic approach being undertaken to design and develop programs by the various CPE stakeholders.

As Houle (1980) equips, ultimately every planner of a CPE program must remain in control of whatever process, principle, or pattern he or she finds useful. Providers C, E and F have found that there are too many similar professional bodies catering for the same members. Their suggestion is to merge the various bodies or share the resources. This would save cost and manpower and provide for a more efficient and effective support system.

As for program development strategies, a suggestion was made to collaborate among the professional bodies instead of duplicating the programs and have poor attendance that results in losing money in the venture. Even though planning frameworks are successful, no continuing educator shares this framework with others. They are influenced by their own personal values and beliefs and the institutional context they work in. Cervero and Schon (1988) encourage CPE educators to be reflective practitioners, if they want to be engaged in this important task.

Provider I also emphasizes that the leader should have sound knowledge of what is happening in the world so that the CPE programs introduced are related to business needs that meet the current challenge. However, the challenge faced by public CPE providers compared to the commercial providers is that whether universities and further education establishments as well as commercial learning providers look set to reap the rewards of providing CPE should they be able to demonstrate the flexibility necessary to meet this adult learning agenda.

Program Administration and Evaluation – Collaborative Relationship

Brookfield (1986) argues that professional providers are skeptics and usually do not want to collaborate. Personal conflicts, political factors, resources and budgetary constraints constantly alter neatly conceived plan of actions. Even though planning frameworks are successful, no continuing educator shares this framework with others. They are influenced by their own personal values and beliefs and the institutional context they work in.

Cervero (1988) states that evaluation processes must be part of the larger cycle of program development; just as program development is a form of professional practice. Evaluation problems like program planning problems are encountered in situations that are characterized by uniqueness uncertainty, and value conflicts. Providers and continuing educators, by using examples from their work place setting can determine the evaluation problems to be solved as well as how to solve them

Houle (1980) tells us to let the various providers do what seems best and the test of the marketplace will prevail. Current issues are complex and funding is difficult as continuing professional education providers try to meet the needs of the professionals, community, business and the industry. Therefore, collaboration can be very advantageous. Information, ideas and resources can be pooled and duplication and harmful competition can be avoided. In spite of the numerous benefits of collaboration, some relationships have failed to accomplish desired objectives and have been terminated, resulting in negative relationships among participants and providers, frustrations over unproductive investments of time and resources. Beder (1984) identifies four dominant themes that are important for success relationships:

i. Reciprocity-there must be a balance in giving and receiving resources and giving up domain and power. Each participant must perceive that resources less valued are being exchanged for resources that are more valued.

ii. System openness - external relationships should be actively sought, and there should be a receptiveness by external perspectives

iii. Trust and commitment - organizations cannot relinquish autonomy or perpetuate their collaborative relationship without trust and commitment. The level of trust and commitment can be affected by history of past collaborative efforts and the styles and personalities of the people involved.

iv. Structures - the compatibility of organizational structures and cultures is an important factor. Flat and flexible organizational structures helps partners adapt to one another and creates an environment of openness and receptivity.

Personal Factors

The people participating in collaborative relationships will contribute to its success or failure. The summary of a study that explored the benefits and problems of the collaboration of 247 organizations (Hohmann, 1985) identifies the individual behaviors of administrators as having significant consequences. The following behaviors characterize administrators who are effective collaborators:

a. The ability to recognize the value and bargaining power of resources at hand and to identify outsiders who can contribute needed resources, the willingness to serve on committees and board outside their organizations and develop networks that could lead to collaboration opportunities, inclusive of planning and organizing skills.

b. Individuals designated to represent an organization in collaboration, profoundly influence their organization's perception of the relationship since information will be evaluated, interpreted and selectively communicated at the individual's discretion, and these representatives communicate frequently with their organizations and are very influential in decision-making processes.

Importance of CPE

There has been an increasing recognition for contribution made by providers who have organized CPE programs. Within this context, the contribution of training and development in general and the professional development of the employees in particular has gained recognition. There has been a consistent growth in both managerial and professional employment.

Many employees belong to professional bodies, which seek to encourage or require members to demonstrate evidence of CPE being defined by Madden and Mitchell (1993) as the maintenance and enhancement of the knowledge, expertise and competence of professionals throughout their careers, according to a plan formulated with regards to the needs of the professional, the employer, the professions and society. The use of the word 'competence' in the context of CPE practice implies an outcome in terms of performance. It is worthy to note that this definition explicitly recognizes the employing organization as a stakeholder in the CPE process. By engaging in development activities, the professional is expected to demonstrate an ability to perform to acceptable standards over a period of time, having regard to the changes and challenges, which accompany all business and organizational activity.

Houle (1980) equips that too few professionals continue to learn throughout their lives. They must be identified and eagerly sought, and this fact permeates and will long continue to permeate the practice of CPE. The effective facilitation of learning is the goal whereby all CPE educators and organization should strive for. Learning will occur when professionals participate in activities that are potentially educative and seen as enhancing their knowledge, skills; like reading, peer review, reflection on practice and formal courses.

There also needs to be support by the organization. In this context, it is viewed that all professional development activities should be effectively managed in relation to the overall organizational business objectives. This consideration encourages and justifies the allocation of resources and general organizational support for CPE. Unless resources for development are unlimited, the potential conflict between these two perspectives may become a concern. An organization with only limited funds to support development will need a coherent framework in order to ensure that their resources are allocated in the best possible way. It is also necessary to determine whether individual development needs accord with business imperatives and therefore CPE becomes a shared responsibility between the individual and the organization.

Ownership of CPE

Lifespan of knowledge gained in an initial degree or professional course declines, and the need for continuing education becomes more urgent. Education and training must become a continuous lifelong process to keep abreast of change. All professionals need a blend of professional and managerial skills. Competencies will vary from individual to individual and according to individual stages of development within the profession. With the rapid change taking place in the industry, professionals are expected to have cross-functional skills acquired through a wide range of business and workplace situations. In this context, Schon (1987) sees two processes at work: knowing in action and reflection in action:

> "...knowing in action would describe the cognitive skills needed to do a job and reflection in action needs the rethinking of some part of knowing in action; which leads to on the spot experimentation and further thinking, that affects what we do in the situation at hand and perhaps also in others, we shall see as similar to it. As such a professional's knowing in action is embedded in the socially and institutionally structured context shared by a community of practitioners"

According to Winter (1996), a key principle for professional competence is that professionalism isn't just about acquiring 'codified knowledge' but depends on 'reflection in action' in the company of other professionals. He further summaries the characteristics of professional work that include involving a situation in which knowledge within a group is pooled but recognized as incomplete and requiring the collaboration of the whole group through a process of reflection relating to the issue or problem. The group arrives at an extension to the knowledge it possesses and recognizes the responsibilities and rights of all parties involved. The group is sensitive to everybody in the group and the group possesses recognized knowledge and expertise which members are able to draw from a wide range of separate experiences. In defining the characteristic of what it means to be a professional, it is the social context in which professionals have their practice.

Individuals play an important part in managing CPE, to enhance oneself in the business and workplace environment. In order to get them started with CPE, individuals need to undertake an audit, set objectives, identify the knowledge and the expertise needed matching existing expertise against current position and identifying gaps. To this extent, Heron (1997) equips that the premise of learning is a social process development of oneself and it can only be realized in and through developing with others.

Individuals need to take risks and move out of their comfort zone thus gaining extraordinary benefit of systematic reflection. Professionals use their practical knowledge to construct their understanding of current situations of practice. This process of thinking in action has been variously called reflection in action (Schon, 1983). As such, CPE is based on the same underlying principles stating that development is owned and managed by the learner and that it is an essentially a personal matter. Summed up aptly by Adam and Plumridge (1995) as those responsible for supporting the growth and development of others in the organization are themselves actively engaged in their own self development, they cannot actually tune in to the quality of the experiences of self developing others.

Planning CPE Programs and Updates

The planning of CPE is generally an issue yet to be recognized as an activity worthy of management time by the providers.

This lack of recognition is evidenced by several tendencies.

i.   There were frequently an absence of coherent CPE policy or a set of CPE objectives that reflect the professional providers driven needs. CPE is perceived as just a special type of development activity.

ii. Records of CPE activity, even where these were maintained, tended to be simplistic with an emphasis on listing development inputs rather than development outcomes.

iii. Few professional providers attempted any form of evaluation of company sponsored professional development.

iv. The major focus of CPE was on external development activity or generic in nature and little thought was applied to the effective management of the learning environment at work.

v.   Most of the providers were unable to cost professional development in terms of either time or finance.

vi. Universities, further education establishments as well as commercial learning providers look set to reap the rewards of providing CPE should they be able to demonstrate the flexibility necessary to meet this adult learning agenda. One of the implications seen in the research is professional institutions and providers either clash or complement ownership of the process of providing CPE, maybe they should look into collaborative efforts to share resources and cost.

vii. CPE programs organized by the continuing providers need to be evaluated, currently most of the programs are run on a generic basis.

Cervero, Pennington and Green (1988) describes that there are four major discrepancies why the above happens:

i.   Little comprehensive needs assessment was done due to a lack of time, expertise or resources, although many planners and providers give lip-service to the importance of needs assessment and very few followed through

ii. There were little evidence that available resources were tapped to determine the program's objectives

iii. There were no indication that the design of instruction was based on the learner characteristics, desired outcomes, time and money or other available resources

iv. After the program was given, comprehensive evaluations were simply not done.

CPE and Collaborative Relationship

Providers need to look at current issues and funding, which is difficult to meet the needs of the community, business and industry. Information, ideas, and resources can be pooled, and duplication and competition can be minimized if collaborations are successful. In this context, collaboration could be seen as a major agency expansion strategy. Partners can provide useful information on needs assessments and program development and evaluation, suggestions for curriculum development, enrollment of participants, use of facilities and state of the art equipment, sharing of staff expertise and additional revenue from increased enrollments of funding.

On the other hand, Cervero (1988) indicates that while there is general agreement that collaborative relationship is good to the point where it is even a 'politically correct' idea, the central question is always: 'who's in charge?' This governance issue is always negotiated in partnerships and the central issues typically revolve around:

1) Who controls the content of the program? and
2) How will profits and losses be shared? These enduring issues are being played out in the CPE agenda. Thus, effective partnerships will develop not from a belief that collaboration is the right thing to do, but from a definitive understanding of the goals to be achieved by the partnership, a clear recognition of the benefits to be gained by each institution, and the contribution of equivalent resources by each partner (Cervero, 1988).

References

Abdul Kadir, Taha. (1981). *Universitipertanianmalaysiadalammelahirkan guru_- guru Professional: SatuTinjauanAwal.*Serdang: UniversitiPertanian Malaysia.

Abrahamson, S. (1984) Evaluation of continuing education in health professions: The state of the art.*Evaluation and the health professions,* 1984, 7, 3 – 23.

Abrams. R. (2003). *The successful business plan: Secrets and strategies* (4th ed.), Palo Alto, CA:Planning Shop

Abramson, P.R. (1992) *A case for case study.* Thousand Oaks, Calif : Sage.

Abrussese, R. S. (1987). The cervero model, *The Journal of Continuing Education in Nursing.*16, 85-88.

Ackoff., R. L. (1974). *Redesigning the future : A systems approach to societal problems.* New York : John Wiley.

Adler, M. (1982). Why only adults can be educated.In Ronald Gross (ed.), *Invitation to lifelong learning.* Chicago: Follet Publishing. 88-103.

Adler, P.A. and Adler, P. (1987). *Membership roles in field research,* Newbury Park, CA: Sage.

Apps, J. W. (1979). *Problems in continuing education.* New York: Mc-Graw-Hill.

Apps, J. W (1985).*Improving practice in continuing education*. San Francisco: Jossey - Bass.

Apps, J. W. (1989). Providers of adult and continuing education: A framework. In . S. B.Merriamand P. M. Cunningham (eds.), *Handbook of adult and continuingeducation*, 275-286. San Francisco: Jossey-Bass

Argyris, C., &Schon, D. A.(1974). *Theory in practice: Increasing professional effectiveness*. San Francisco: Jossey-Bass.

Argyris, C., &Schon, A. Donald (1974). *Theory in practice.*San Francisco: Jossey-Bass.

Azzaretto, J. F. (1987). Competitive strategy in continuing professional education.

In C. Bader (ed.), Competitive strategies for continuing education – *New Direction for Continuing Education*. 35. San Francisco: Jossey-Bass.

Baehr, M. (1984). The empirical link between program development and performance needs of professionals and executives. *Continuum*, 48 (3).

Barber, B. (1963). Inter-organizational relations: A review of the field. *Journal of Higher Education*, 52, 1 – 28.

Baskett, H. K. (2000). Research in university continuing education is dead: Long live reflective practice. *Canadian Journal of University Continuing Education.*22. 2. Fall.

Becker, H.S. (1962). The nature of a profession, In N.B. Nelson (ed.), *Educations for the professions*. Chicago: University of Chicago Press.

Benner, P. (1984). *From novice to expert: Excellence and power in clinical nursing practice*. Menlo Park, CA: Addison – Wesley.

Benson, A. (2001). Planning and implementing on-line degree systems: *A case study of statewide university system distance learning Iniative.* Unpublished doctoral dissertation, University of Georgia.

Berg, B.L. (1983). *Qualitative research methods for social sciences.,* Allyn& Bacon, U.S.A.

Black, R., & Schell, J. (1995). Learning with a situated cognition framework. implications for adult learning. Paper Presented at the AVAC, Co. *ERIC documentreproduction service.* 389 - 939.

Bloom, G.F. (1983). The real estate professional. In M.R. Stern (ed.), *Power and conflict in continuing professional education.* Belmont, Calif: Wadsaorth.

Bogdan, R., &Anor (1992). *Qualitative research for education: An introduction to theory and methods.* Allyn& Bacon, U.S.A.

Bogdan, R.C., &Biklen, S.K (1992). *Qualitative research for education: An introduction to theory and methods.*Needham Heights, MA: Allyn and Bacon.

Boone, E. J. (1985). *Developing programs in adult education.* Prentice Hall, Inc, USA.

Boyle, P.G. (1981) *Planning better programs.*McGraw-Hill Book, Inc.

Broad, M.L., &Newstrom, J.W. (1992) *Transfer of training.* Reading, MA: Addison -Wesley.

Bromfield, K. (1998). *CPD and WIFM.* Emerging issues in continuing professional development. Internet Conference.

Brookfield, S.D (1986). *Understanding and facilitating adult learning.* San Francisco, Jossey-Bass.

Bryman, A., & Burgess, R.G. (1994). *Analyzing qualitative data.*Routledge, London.

Burgess, R.G. (1984).*In the field: An introduction to field research*, London: Allen andUrwin.

Burnes, B. (1996). *Managing change.* Pitman Publishing, UK.

Butcher, R., & Strauss, A. (1961). Professions in process.*American Journal of Sociology.*

Caffarella, R.S. (1994). *Planning programs for adult learners: A practical guide for educators, trainers, and staff developers.* Jossey-Bass Inc. USA.

Campbell, D. D. (1977). *Adult education as a field of study and practice: Strategies for development.* Vancouver: The University of Columbia and the International Council of Education.

Cervero, R.M. (1984). Collaboration in university continuing professional education. In H.W.Beder (ed.), Realising the potential of inter-organizational co-operation. *New directions for continuing education*, no 23. San Francisco:Jossey Bass

Cervero, R.M. (1985*).* Continuing professional education and behavior change; A model of research and evaluation.*The Journal of Continuing Education in Nursing.*

Cervero, R.M., Rottet, S., &Dimmock, K.H. (1986). Analyzing the effectiveness of continuing professional education at the workplace.*Adult Education Quarterly.*

Cervero, R.M., & Young, W.H. (1987). The organization and provision of continuing professional education : A critical review and synthesis In J.C. Smart (ed.), Higher education : *Handbook of theory and research.* 3. New York :Agathon Press.

Cervero, R.M. (1988). *Effective continuing education for professional.* Jossey-Bass, San Francisco.

Cervero, R.M., &Azzaretto, J.F. (1990). *Visions for the future of continuing professional education.* Athens: Georgia Centre for Continuing Education, University of Georgia.

Cervero, R. M. (1993). *Planning responsibility for adult education.* San Francisco: Jossey-Bass

Cervero, R. M., & Wilson, A. L.(1994). *Planning responsibly for adult education.* San Francisco: Jossey-Bass

Cervero, R.M. (2000). Trends and issues in continuing professional education. New directions for adult and continuing education. 86 : 1 – 12. OCLC FirstSearch : Full text. retrieved 26 September 2002. *http: // newfirstsearch.oclc.org*

Cervero, R. M. (2001). Continuing professional education in transition, 1981-2000. *International Journal of Lifelong Education,* 20 (1/2),16-30.

Clarke, L. (1994). *The essence of change.* Prentice Hall Int., UK.

Clyne, S. (1995).*Continuing professional development.* Kogan Page Ltd.

Cross,K.P. (1981). *Adults as learners: Increasing participation and facilitating learning.* San Francisco: Jossey-Bass

Cruse, R.B. (1983).The accounting profession.In M.R. Stern (ed) *Power and conflict in continuing professional education.* Belmont, Calif: Wadsworth.

Cyrs, T. E., Jr.(1978). *Design of a competency-determined curriculum model for pharmacy education.* Chicago: Office of Continuing Education, The University of Chicago

Daley, B, (2001). Learning and professional practice.*Adult Education Quarterly* 50, 4 . 243-272

Daley, J. (2004). Learning and context : Connections in continuing professional education. *Advances in Developing Human Resources.* 6. 1, 86 – 100, Sage Publications,

Darkenwald, G. G., & Merriam, S.B. (1982). *Adult education: Foundations of practice.* New York: Harper.

Dave, R.H. (1976). *Foundations of lifelong education.* Oxford :Pergamon Press (Eds.)

Davis, S., &Botkin, J. (1994). *The monster under the bed: How business is mastering the opportunity of knowledge for profit.* New York: Simon & Schuster.

Day, H.P. (1980) How do you translate continuing education. *Adult Leadership.* 22 (2), 73 – 74.

Denzin, N. K. (1994). *Handbook of qualitative research.*Sage Publications, U.S.A.

Dewey, J. (1933). *How we think.* Lexington, Mass. : Heath, 1933.

Dreyfus, H.L., & Dreyfus, S. E. (1986) *Mind over machine.* Oxford, England : Basil Balckwell.

Fryer, B.V. (1962). Lifetime learning for physicians: Principles, practices, proposals. *Journal of Medicine Education,* 37 (2).

Fingeret, A. (1984).Who's in control? A Case study of university industry cooperation. In H.W. Beder (ed.), Realizing the potential of inter-organizational co-operation.*New directions for continuing education,* 23. San Francisco :Jossey-Bass.

Firestone, W.A. (1987). Meaning in method: The rhetoric of quantitative and qualitative research. *Educational Reseacher,* 16(7), 16 – 21.

Flexner, A. (1915)Is social work a profession. *School and Society.*

Flexner, A. (1975)Is social work a profession. *School and Society*, 1, 901 – 911.

Fletcher, S. (1998). *Competence and organizational change.*Kogan Page Ltd.

Flint, B. (1961). *Program development in the Louisiana co-operative extension service.* Louisiana state university and agriculture and mechanical college.

Fox, R.D. (1981). Formalorganizational structure and participation in planning continuing professional education.*Adult Education Quarterly*, 31, 209 – 226.

Fox, R. D. (1983). Discrepancy analysis in continuing medical education-A conceptual model. *Mobius.* 3, (3).

Fox, R. D. (1984). Fostering transfer of learning to work environments. In T. J. Sork (ed.), Designing and implementing effective workshops. *New directions for adult and continuing education.* 22. San Francisco:Jossey-Bass

Franks, T., & Cruickshank, I. (2001). Evolutionary pressure: The history of CPD in the USA. Continuing professional development: *California Spins.* Issue 5,

Freire, P. (1970). *Pedagogy of the oppressed.*trans. Myra Bergman Ramos. NY: Seabury.

Friedson, E. (1986).*Professional power.* Chicago: University of Chicago Press, Fritz, F. (1991) *Creating.* New York : Fawcett Columbine.

Garfinkel, H. (1967). *Studies in ethnomethodology.* Eaglewood Cliffs, NJ : Prentice Hall.

Glacken, J. (1981). *Continuing education: Mandatory or voluntary?* Unpublished Papers from Rutgers university graduate school of education.

Glaser, B.G., & Strauss, A.L. (1967).*The discovery of grounded theory.* Chicago, Aldine, 1967.

Glaser, B.G., & Strauss, A.L. (1973). *The discovery of grounded theory : Strategies for qualitative research.* Chicago: Aldine.

Glaser, B.G. (1978). *Theoretical sensitivity.* Mill Valley, Calif: Sociology Press,

Glesne, C., &Peshkin, A. (1992). *Becoming qualitative researchers: An introduction.* White Plain, NY:Longman.

Goetz. J.P., & LeCompte, M.D. (1984). *Ethnography and qualitative design in educational research.* Orlando, Fla: Academic Press.

Griffin, L.J. (1993). Narrative event structure analysis and causal interpretation in historical sociology. *American Journal of Sociology.* 98; 1094 – 1133.

Guba, E.G., & Lincoln, Y.S. (1981). *Effective evaluation.* San Francisco: Jossey-Bass.

Guba, E., &Lincoln,Y. (1989).*Fourth generation evaluation.* Newbury Park, CA: Sage.

Hall, G. E., & Jones, H. L. (1976). *Competency-based education; A process for improvement of education.* Englewood Cliffs, NJ:Prentice-Hall

Hemmings, M.B. (1984) *Next steps in public – private partnership.* (eds.), 253 – 702.

Heron, J. (1997). *Catharsis in human development.*Potential Research Society, University of Surrey.

Horne, Esther. E. (1985).*Continuing education: Issues and challenges.*Library and information science professions.

Houle, C.O. (1972). *The design of education.* San Francisco: Jossey-Bass.

Houle, C.O. (1980). *Continuing learning in the professions.*Jossey-Bass, San Francisco, USA.

Houle, C.O. (1983). Possible futures. In M.R. Stern (ed.), *Power and conflict in continuing professional education.* Belmont, Calif: Wadsworth.

Illich, I. (1977). *Disabling professions.* London: Martin Boyers.

Institute of Personnel and Development, (1984). *The HMSO training report.* London.

Jarvis, P (1987). *Adult learning in the social context.* London: Croom Helm

Jarvis, P (1999). *The practitioner-researcher: Developing theory from practice.* San Francisco: Jossey Bass.

Jones, N., & Robinson, R. (1998). Do organizations manage continuing professional development. *Journal of Management Development*, 16, 3.

Kenny, J., Donnelly, E., & Reid, M. (1979) *Manpower training and development: An Introduction,* (2nd ed.), London: Institute of Personnel Management.

Kenny, J.B. (1982). Competency analysis for trainers: A model for professionalization. *Training & Development Journal*, 36(5) 142 – 148.

Kenny, W.R. (1985). Program planning and accreditation. In R.M. Cervero and C. L. Scarlan (eds.), Problems and prospects in continuing professional education – *New direction for continuing education*, 27, San Francisco: Jossey Bass.

Kerka, S. (1994).Mandatory continuing education.*ERIC Digest*, 151.

Kidder, L.H. (1981).*Research methods in social relations.* Austin, T., Holt R. and Winston.

Knowles, M.S. (1975). *Self directed learning.* New York: Association Press.

Knowles, M.S. (1980). *The modern practice of adult education*: Andragogy versus pedagogy (rev. ed.). Englewood Cliffs, NJ: Prentice-Hill.

Knowles, M.S. (1980) *The modern practice of adult education*. Chicago: Association Press.

Knowles, M. (1984). *The adult learners: A neglected species*. (3rd ed.). Houston: Gulf Publishing.

Knowles, M. (1990). *The adult learners: A neglected species*. (rev. ed.). Houston: Gulf Publishing.

Knox, A. B. (1979). Assessing the impact of continuing education.(eds.),*New directions for continuing education*, 3. San Francisco :Jossey-Bass.

Knox, A.B. (1981). The continuing education agency and its parent organization. In J.C. Votruba (ed.), Strengthening internal support for continuing education. *New directions for continuing education*, 9. San Francisco :Jossey-Bass.

Knox, A.B. (1986). *Helping adult learn*. San Francisco: Jossey-Bass.

Knox, A. B. (1987). Reducing barriers to participation in continuing education. *LifelongLearning: An Omnibus of Practice and Research*. 10, 7-9.

Larson, M.S. (1979).*The rise of professionalism: A sociologic analysis*. University of California Press, Berkeley.

Lengrand, J. P. (1975). *Program planning to meet people's needs, extension_ education in community development. Directorate of extension.*Ministry of food and agriculture, Government of India, New Delhi.

Lengrand, P. (1975). *An introduction to lifelong education*. London: Croom Helm.

Lent, J.A. (1979).*Malaysian studies: Present knowledge and research trends.* Center forasian studies: Northern Illinois University.

Lester, S. (1995) Beyond knowledge and competencies: Towards a framework professional education. *In Capability* UK: Higher Education for Capability. 1 (3), 44 – 52.

Lincoln, Y. S., &Guba, E. G. (1985). *Naturalistic inquiry,* Thousand Oaks. CA:Sage

Lindsay, C. A., Queeny, D. S., &Smutz, W. D. (1981). *A Model of process for university and professional association collaboration.* University Park: Pennsylvania State University

Lofland, J., &Lofland, L.H. (1995). *Social settings: A guide to qualitative* observation and analysis. (3rd ed.). Belmont, Calif: Wadsworth.

Long, H.B. (1983).*Adult learning.* New York: Cambridge University Press.

Maclean, R. G. (1996). Negotiating between Competing interests in planning continuing medical education. In R. Cervero and A. L. Wilson (eds.), What really matters in adult education program planning: Lessons in negotiating and power Interests, 69, 47-58. *New directions for adult and continuing education.* San Francisco, Jossey-Bass.

Malaysian Institute of Estate Agents. (2000) Souvenir program*: Challenges ahead.* 10 -15. Pelanduk Press.

Marshall, C., &Rossman, G.B. (1995). *Designing qualitative research.*(2nd ed.). California, Sage Publishing Inc.

Mattran, (1981). Mandatory education increases professional competence, in *Examiningcontroversies in adult education,* (ed.), 49, B.W. Kreitlow and Associates

Maurer, C., & Sheets, T.E. (1998). Foreword to volume 1, national organizations of the US. *Encyclopedia of Associations.*(33rd ed.).Detroit : Gall Research.

McGuire, C.H., Foley, R.P., Gorr, A. Richards, RW. & Associates (1983). *Handbook health professions education.*Jossey-Bass.

McPherson, G.(1972). *Small town teacher.*Cambridge, MA: Harvard University.

Merriam, S.B., & Brockett, R.G. (1977*). The professional and practice of adult education: An introduction.* San Francisco: Jossey-Bass.

Merrian, S.B. (1998). *Qualitative research & case study in education.* Jossey-Bass Inc. U.S.A.

Merriam, S.B, &Caffarella.(1999*). Learning in adulthood: A comprehensive study .* San Francisco: Jossey-Bass.

Meyer, T.C. (1975). Toward a continuum in medical education. *Bulletin of the New York Academy of Medicine,* 51, 719 – 726.

Miles, M.B. (1994). *Qualitative data analysis: An expanded sourcebook.* Sage Publications, U.S.A.

Mitroff, I.(1983). *Stakeholders of the organizational mind.* San Francisco: Jossey-.Bass

Mott, V., & Daley, B. J. (2000). Charting a course for continuing professional education: Reframing professional practice. (eds.), *New directions for adult and continuing education,* 84. San Francisco: Jossey-Bass

Mullins, L.J. (1996). *Management and organizational behavior.* Pitman Publishing

Mumford, A. (1997). *Action learning at work.*Aldershot: Gower.

Nadler, D. A.(1998). *Champions for change: How CEO's and their companies are mastering the skills of radical change.* San Francisco: Jossey-Bass.

Nasseh, B. (1999). Continuing professional education models. Retrieved on 25 June 2005. *www. bsu.edu/classes/nasseh/profess.html.*

Nowlen, P.M., & Stern, M. S. (1981). Partnership in continuing education for professionals. In American Association For Higher Education. (ed.), *Partnerships with business and the professions.* Washington D.C.: American Association For Higher Education.

Nowlen, P.M. (1988). *A new approach to continuing education for business and the professions, the performance model.* Macmillan, New York.

O'Niel, J. (1999). *The role of advisors in action learning*: Unpublished Dissertation Teachers' College Columbia University, New York.

Parson, T. (1949).*Essays in sociology theory.* New York : Free Press.

Patton, M.Q. (1985). *Quality in qualitative research: Methodical principles and recent development.* Invited address to division J of the American educational research association, Chicago, April, 1985 .

Patton, M.Q. (1990). *Qualitative evaluative methods,* Thousand Oaks Calf: Sage.

Pedler, M. (1997). *Action learning in practice.*(3rd ed.), Brookfiled VT: Gower.

Pennington, F.C. & Green, J. (1976). Comparative analysis of program development processes in six professions.*Adult Education Quartely, 27,* 13-21

Polanyi, M. (1967). *The tacit dimension.* New York. Anchor.

Punch, M. (1986). *The politics and ethics of fieldwork.* Newbury Park, CA: Sage.

Queeney, D.S. (2000). Continuing professional education. In A.L. Wilson & E.R. Hayes. (eds.), *Handbook of adult and continuing education.* 375 – 391, San Francisco, Jossey-Bass.

Ram, I. (1998). Re: CPO and personal commitment. Emerging issues in continuing professional development. internet conference. Retrieved on 1 August 2002. *http://www.openhouse.orguk/virtual-university-press/cpd/*

Revans, R.W. (1982). *The origins and growth of action learning.* Bickly, Kent, Chartwell-Bratt and Lund; Swenden: Studenlitteratur.

Rivera, W.M. (1982*). Reflections on policy issues in adult education.Issues in continuing for adults*,1, : *Policy issues and process.* Department of agriculture and extension education, University of Maryland at College Park.

Rockhill, (1981). Professional education should not be mandatory in *Examining controversies in adult education,* (ed.), 62. B.W. Kreitlow and Associates.

Rogers, E.M. (1995). *Diffusion of innovations.* New York: Free Press.

Schon, D.A. (1971). *Beyond the stable state.* New York. Anchor.

Schon, D.A. (1975). Deutero – learning in organizations. Learning for increased effectiveness. *Organizational Dynamics.* 3, 3 – 16.

Schon, D.A. (1983). *The reflective practitioner.*New York:Basic Books.

Schon, D.A. (1987*). Educating the reflective practitioner.* San Francisco: Jossey Bass.

Schon, D.A. (1996). From technical rationality to reflection-in-action. In R. Edwards Hanson and P. Raggatt (eds.). *Boundaries of adult learning.* London: Rontledge.

Senge, P. (1990*). The fifth discipline: The art and practice of the learning organization*. New York: Doubleday.

Shamsuddin Ahmad. (1995). *Contextual factors associated with evaluation practicesof selected adult and continuing education providers in Malaysia*. Unpublished doctoral dissertation .University of Georgia, Athens.

Sheila, M. Date (1985). *Approaches from a distance: Some thoughts on distance education in the continuing education of librarians*, Conference Publications, New York.

Smutz, W.D. Crowe, M.B., & Lindsay, C.A. (1986). Emerging perspectives on continuing professional education. In J.C. Smart (ed.). Higher Education :*Handbook of theory & research*. 2. New York: Agathon Press.

Sork, T.J., &Caffarella, R.S. (1989).Planning programs for adults.In S.B. Merriam (eds.), *Handbook of adult and continuing education*, 233 – 245. San Francisco, Jossey- Bass

Sork, T.J. &Caffarella, R.S. (1994). Planning programs for adults: *Handbook of adult and continuing education*.Jossey Bass Publishers.

Stake, R.E. (1994). Case studies. In N.K. Denzin and V.S. Lincoln, (eds.). *Handbook ofqualitative research*. Thousand Oaks, Calif: Sage, 1994.

Stake, R. (1995). *The art of case research:* Thousand Oaks, Sage Publications, U.S.A.

Stone,E.W. (1986).*The growth of continuing education*.Library Trends. 450-455.

Strauss, A.S., & Corbin, J. (1990). *Basics of qualitative research: Grounded theory and techniques*. Sage Publications Inc. U.K.

Stubblefield, H. W. (1981). What should be the focus of adult education? The focus should be on life fulfilment. In B. Kreitlow (ed.), *Examining controversies in adult education, 12-13*. San Francisco: Jossey-Bass.

Suleiman, A. (1983). Private enterprise:The independent provider. In M.R.Stern (ed.), *Power and conflict in continuing professional education*. Belmont, Calif : Wadsworth.

Taylor, S.J, &Bogdan, R.C. (1984). *Introduction to qualitative research and methods*. The search for meaning, New York, Wiley.

Titmus, C.J. (1989). *Lifelong education for adults: An international hand book*. Pergamon Press, U.K.

Todd, F. (1987). *Planning continuing professional development*. Croom Helm, Beckenham, England.

Toombs, W., & Lindsay, C. (1985). Modifying faculty roles to institutionalize continuing professional education.*Research in Higher Education*, 22, 93 – 109.

True, W.R. & True, J.H. (1977). *Street ethnography*. Beverly Hills.CA: Sage.

Tyler, R.W. (1949). *Principles of curriculum and instruction*. Chicago: University of Chicago Press.

Umble, K.E., &Cervero, R.M.(1996). Impact studies in continuing education for health professionals : A critique of research syntheses. *Evaluation and the Health Professions*. 19, 2, 148-174.

Umble, K.E., Cervero, R.M. &Langone, C.A. (2001).Negotiating about power frames and continuing education: A case study in public health. *Adult Education Quarterly*, 57(2), 128 – 145.

Valentine, T. (1984). The consequences of mismanaged interagency collaborations. *New directions continuing education*, (23), 65.

Van Maanen, J. (1979). *Qualitative methodology*.Sage Publications, U.S.A.

Vaughan, P. (1991). *Maintaining professional competence*. Department of Adult Education, University of Hull.

Vernon, D.H. (1983). Education for proficiency : The continuum. *Journal of Legal Education,* 33, 559 – 569.

Vollmer, H.M., & Mills, D.L. (1966). *Professionalization.* Eaglewood, Cliffs, N.J.: Prentice Hall.

Walker, R. L. (1985). *Applied qualitative research.* Gower Publishing Co. Ltd., U.K.

Winter, R. (1996).*Professional competence and higher education* : The Asset Program, Falmer Press.

Wolcott, H.F. (1992). *The Handbook of qualitative research in education.* Orlando, Fla: Academic Press.

Yin, R. (1994).*Case study research: Design & methods.,* Sage Publishing, CA.

Young, W.H.(1998). *Continuing professional education in Transition.* Malabar, Fla: Krieger.